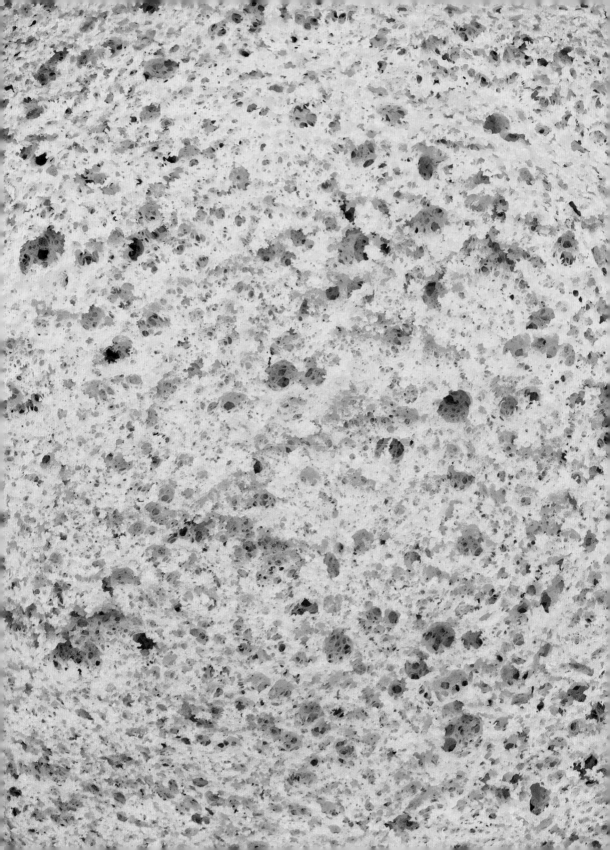

Tom Oxford & Oliver Coysh

BAKE IT EASY

One-pan Recipes That Prove Baking is a Piece of Cake

photography by Sam A Harris

quadrille

For Ernest & Kingsley

Quadrille, Penguin Random House UK, One Embassy Gardens, 8 Viaduct Gardens, London SW11 7BW

Quadrille Publishing Limited is part of the Penguin Random House group of companies whose addresses can be found at global.penguinrandomhouse.com

Text © Thomas Oxford & Oliver Coysh 2025
Photography © Sam A Harris 2025
Illustrations © Ailsa Johnson 2022
Design and layout © Quadrille 2025

Thomas Oxford and Oliver Coysh have asserted their right to be identified as the author(s) of this Work in accordance with the Copyright, Designs and Patents Act 1988

Published by Quadrille in 2025

www.penguin.co.uk

A CIP catalogue record for this book is available from the British Library

ISBN 978 1 83783 260 6
10 9 8 7 6 5 4 3 2 1

Colour reproduction by F1

Printed in China by C&C Offset Printing Co., Ltd

The authorised representative in the EEA is Penguin Random House Ireland, Morrison Chambers, 32 Nassau Street, Dublin DO2 YH68.

Penguin Random House is committed to a sustainable future for our business, our readers and our planet. This book is made from Forest Stewardship Council® certified paper.

Managing Director Sarah Lavelle
Senior Commissioning Editor Stacey Cleworth
Assistant Editor Sofie Shearman
Designer Katy Everett
Photographer Sam A Harris
Photographer's Assistant Matt Hague
Brand Consultant Will Perrens
Illustrator Ailsa Johnson
Props Stylist Max Robinson
Food Stylist Becks Wilkinson
Food Stylist Assistant Valeria Russo
Head of Production Stephen Lang
Production Manager Sabeena Atchia

INTRODUCTION

SWEET TIMES

When we got the nod to write our second baking book, we were both excited and a little apprehensive. We'd put so much into the first book, *Bake It. Slice It. Eat It.*, that we thought we might have used up all our ideas. This proved to be completely untrue. Once we got down to business, we realised there was loads more creative batter left in the bowl, along with plenty of spare baking knowledge to throw into the mix.

If you read our first book, then welcome back. If you didn't, we're not annoyed, just disappointed. Disappointed you didn't get to try all of the tasty treats it had to offer! In this book, we go a little slower – taking it easy. Sticking to our belief that baking should always be fun, accessible and enjoyably unpredictable, we've stripped things back, flung the kitchen doors wide open and invited everyone to join the party. So, whether you're a kitchen newbie or a veteran oven jockey, we're here to gently rock your baking world. We embrace the imperfections,

celebrate the substitutions and hail the glorious mess that is home baking. We're trading stiff peaks for easy beats, and whipping up a storm that's about taste, not waste. We're advocating for ingredients that don't cost the earth, metaphorically and literally, ensuring you won't have to sell a kidney to afford a slice of delicious cake.

This book is bursting with ideas that'll have you rifling through your cupboards in a rush to get your bake on. This book is a celebration of real cake that exists to be devoured, that tastes like home and conjures memories of sticky fingers and licked spoons. Cake that doesn't demand a dedicated baking room, but lives and thrives in the heart of your home, or even the great outdoors. There's no need for precision or perfection here. All you need is a hankering for good cake and a desire to have fun. It's time to crank up your oven, don your apron and *Bake It Easy*.

A LITTLE ABOUT US

We're Tom and Ollie, and we started the Exploding Bakery all the way back in 2011. Built on a love of cake, an idea of how it should be made and some seriously low-budget equipment, the Exploding Bakery burst into life in the form of a tiny cafe in Devon.

Remembering the early days keeps us in touch with the values we started with, which were to always bring an element of fun to baking, keep things as simple as possible and concentrate on the ingredients, flavour and texture, so the cakes can speak for themselves. Thinking back also reminds us how much our business has grown and evolved: our cakes are now stocked in Fortnum & Mason, we have a flourishing online cake shop and on the wholesale side of the business, we are hand-making millions of slices to supply to other cafes, delis and farm shops across the country. Seeing how far we've come is a reminder of the most important lesson for any small business – how to survive and thrive.

We're still the best of friends and see this friendship as the beating heart of the Exploding Bakery – maybe that's because we can regress a little at work and bring some of that schoolyard playfulness into what we do every day.

SOME WORDS FROM OLIVER

Sometimes I feel like I'm in a toxic relationship with cake. After we finished the first book, I needed a break. I'd put on quite a bit of weight and lost my appetite for all things sweet. During recipe testing I'd have to eat five or six slices of cake – I'd forgo lunch and sometimes dinner. It felt like this passion for cake was now eating me from the inside out and I needed a bit of space to truly rekindle my love for baking.

There's something surreal about falling out of love with a creation as perfect as cake. The kitchen that was once my sanctuary started to feel like a battleground, littered with the casualties of empty flour sacks on the floor and the splatter of cake mix up the wall. I would stand there, whisk in hand, feeling more like a soldier than a baker. But, as with all great loves, absence made the heart grow fonder. The break I took wasn't just necessary; it was transformative. It allowed me to rediscover myself beyond the oven mitts and baking trays.

This time round I've really got my sweet tooth back, with a crazed look in my eye like the cookie monster, devouring everything that comes out of the oven like there's no tomorrow. The clatter of the whisk against the bowl was no longer a battle cry but a symphony for good things to come. The oven's warmth returned as a comforting embrace, and the scent of fresh bakes made my heart flutter once more.

SOME WORDS FROM TOM

When our first book was done and dusted, I found myself abruptly catapulted back into the daily grind of running our bakery and cafe. It was like coming down from a sugar high, only to face a barrage of practicalities: fixing broken freezers, wrestling with giant new ovens and staring down the barrel of marketing meetings and spreadsheet marathons. The glitz of book signings quickly faded into the background noise of small business survival.

Then, out of the blue, came the call for a second book. Adjusting my mindset wasn't a walk in the park. Amidst the chaos of daily operations, carving out time to write another one seemed borderline insane. Yet, there was an undeniable thrill to it, and it injected a fresh vitality into how we see our cakes.

We decided to break free from our trusty rectangular tin, which had faithfully served us for 14 years. This new book became our ticket to explore uncharted baking territories, with curvaceous springforms and towering loaf tins as our vessels. The recipes we created for this book inspired us to reimagine our cake range. New cakes for wholesale and, yes, even the audacious debut of round cakes.

When it came to putting pen to paper, or rather, buttery fingers to keyboard, Oliver and I slipped effortlessly back into our writing groove. Our recipe testing sailed smoothly, buoyed by a shiny new test kitchen and the invaluable addition of Beth, a baking virtuoso who joined our team at precisely the right moment. We owe much of our success to her steady hand and creative flair.

In the end, writing our second book wasn't just about recipes, it was about rediscovering the joy of creation amidst the flour clouds and chaos, and realizing that sometimes, the sweetest surprises come when you dare to break the familiar cake moulds.

WHY 'THE EXPLODING BAKERY'? It's all about the energy, the colliding of ingredients and flavours and the reaction of those with heat, moisture and acid. We wanted our name to conjure visuals, much like the Big Bang – you can't help but think about the universe and all the energy that brought it into being. Well, we might not be anywhere near that explosive, but it's our own little Big Bang bakery and we're ever-expanding, just like our amazing universe. Whatever it makes you think of, we're probably a bit of that.

This is a baking book that strips away the intricacies and saves you time, so that you can sit back, bake it easy and scoff the fruits of your labour. We want people to love baking at home, so we've continued our mission to demystify it, making it accessible and enjoyable for everyone. We follow the ethos of our first book, *Bake It. Slice It. Eat It.*, and bring you a fresh collection of recipes that are lighter on your bank balance and a little easier on your schedule.

The following are the foundations we laid when we set out to write a recipe book that made baking easy, affordable and a joy, without losing what makes baking special – the fun and the flavour.

AFFORDABLE

This is not always achievable when it comes to buying baking ingredients, as cream, butter, chocolate, nuts and vanilla will often set you back a good chunk of your disposable income. For this book, however, we've deliberately not chosen the luxury ingredients, as we believe you can almost always find an ingredient or alternative to meet your budget. We've also tried to work our recipes around standard packet sizes, so you're not left with half a tub of something that will sit in the fridge for weeks before getting chucked in the bin. If you can't afford the best ingredients, we feel you should still have a go at baking. Learn some skills, enjoy the process and perhaps one day, when you're a seasoned baker, you might be able to afford some Valrhona chocolate for your brownies.

ACCESSIBILITY

All the recipes in this book have been made with ingredients bought from the supermarket. Professional kitchens and bakeries have access to a very wide range of ingredients to help them on their way to consistency, glossy perfection, prolonged shelf life and all the other important parts of commercial baking. We deliberately wanted to avoid using these things, which are bought from wholesale suppliers and specialist shops, instead baking from your perspective, in the real world. That's why you won't find citric acid, stabilisers, emulsifiers or any other gunk in this book. These recipes are designed the Exploding Bakery way – 'cake without the cack'. It's time we all moved away from ultra-processed foods and with home baking, you can control what goes in your food and what goes in your gut.

TIME-SAVING

Each recipe is designed to take up no more than 30 hands-on minutes to get oven ready. These 30 minutes will sometimes be spread over a longer time frame where you dip in and out of the process – you might leave something in the fridge for a few hours or even overnight. In any case, there's more time for you to put your feet up and dream about making all the other recipes in this book.

FEWER INGREDIENTS

We wanted to keep our recipes simple yet packed with flavour, avoiding endless ingredients lists. We believe that simple, honest baking works best if you allow the core ingredients to stand out and shine, meaning you don't always need to add that extra flourish. The fewer ingredients you use, the more you can enjoy the process and get to know the ones you have.

ABOUT THIS BOOK

STORE CUPBOARD

We're championing those forgotten ingredients that lurk deep in your cupboards or stuck to the back of your freezer. We're not just talking about the baking staples such as flour, sugar and eggs here; we're talking about the purgatory of the pantry. That spare jar of cardamom pods gathering dust on the spice rack, the preserve you gamely bought from the Women's Institute stall at a village fête. These are the types of ingredients we want you to lift up like baby Simba on Pride Rock in *The Lion King*. This is their moment.

In this book, we double down on our philosophy of simple, fuss-free baking. We focus instead on the pure pleasure of creating delicious treats. There's no need for a kitchen filled with unused gadgets and gizmos. Instead, we bring you recipes that celebrate the beauty of humble ingredients, transformed into extraordinary flavours and textures.

Let this book be your trusty companion in the kitchen. Its pages will hopefully become a tapestry of memories – smudged with chocolate, dotted with flour and lovingly worn. We urge you to add your personal touch to these recipes, adapting them to your taste and making each bake a unique expression of your creativity. Scribble some notes if you wish. We'd love this book to be truly yours, so take ownership of your favourite recipe and dash across the spongy plains of the cake frontier, planting your very own baking flag.

We hope this book also showcases the humour and easy nature of our friendship, which has spanned more than a quarter of a century and means we are able to inject some of that levity into our baking, writing and day-to-day work. Reading between the lines, we hope it also captures a glimpse of our journey with the Exploding Bakery, and a peek behind the curtain from our humble beginnings in 2011 to a beacon of the cake revolution, teaching us the importance of sticking to our roots while continually innovating and improving.

Bake It Easy is hopefully more than just a collection of recipes; it's a reflection of our growth and our unwavering belief in the power of good, honest baking. It's about returning to basics, appreciating the simplicity of good ingredients and understanding that, sometimes, the simplest things bring the greatest joy.

The title, *Bake It Easy*, encapsulates our approach to baking and to life, especially when you're spending too much time in the fast lane. It's our philosophy that baking doesn't have to be complicated to be rewarding. We chose this title to convey the ease and pleasure that can be found in the kitchen, encouraging both novice and experienced bakers to embrace the joy of creating something beautiful and delicious without the stress. Even for us, baking at home can be like a busman's holiday and it sometimes feels as though we're bringing work home. We're much more likely to bake in our own kitchens when we take a more relaxed approach, so we hope you find that in this book too. Let's have fun, one easy bake at a time.

Each of the recipes is geared towards a certain shape of tin. There's also a handy little illustration next to each one as a quick guide to the suggested tin: square, round or loaf.

SQUARE

20cm x 20cm (8in x 8in). This is usually 5cm (2in) deep and is sometimes referred to as a brownie tin. Easy to find and to use, this is one of the most popular baking tins in the world. We'd recommend getting two tins for ease of lining and baking, though you may find they don't stack too well.

We like the Tala Performance 20cm (8in) square tin – it's made from carbon steel so gives an even bake every time.

ROUND

20cm (8in) loose base, fixed base and/or springform. This should ideally be a minimum of 7cm (2¾in) deep, and can be up to 8cm (3¼in) deep. We'd always recommend using the deeper ones. There are also a few different types, some with loose bases, some without, and the ever-useful springform, which we would recommend if you only have space for one. We use a 20cm (8in) Tala springform cake tin that's 7cm (2¾in) deep, and made of carbon steel for reliable, consistent results.

LOAF

2lb (900g) and approx. 25cm x 15cm x 7.5cm deep (10in x 6in x 3in). We've made everything in a carbon steel Tala 2lb loaf tin.

There really is no standardization on this volume of loaf tin. This is down to the tins needing to accommodate various bread dough recipes, the weight and density of which mean that the tins have myriad dimensions. This is not a problem – whichever tin you use will give a great shape. It just means that you need to keep an eye on the bake times, depending on how deep or shallow your tin is. If things are getting a bit dark on the top, a tin foil canopy will mean you can keep baking without the risk of burning.

If you're using a loaf tin to bake a recipe designed for the round or square tins, we recommend dropping the temperature slightly and baking for an extra 10–15 minutes. The mass of cake mix means it will take longer for the middle to cook.

A NOTE ON THE TINS' MATERIAL
We love steel as it conducts heat in a consistent way that tends not to burn the crust of the cake. Aluminium can be trickier – it conducts heat a little too well and might scorch the cake. Ceramic or glass dishes are rarely good for baking. They take a long time to heat up, then they hold that heat for too long, meaning that they will keep cooking your cake long after it comes out of the oven. Silicone trays sound good in theory, as you don't need to line them, but we're yet to get good results from using them. The silicone just doesn't conduct heat well enough and you tend to end up with a cake without a satisfactory crust. So: stick to steel and you'll be rewarded with an even crumb.

LET'S INTRODUCE THE TINS

In each recipe, we have selected our preferred method for lining the baking tin. Some of the more liquid batters require a watertight lining, while others benefit from a more minimal approach, so it's good to read these techniques before you get mixing.

SCRUNCH-UP METHOD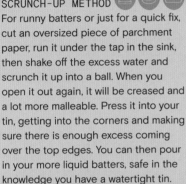
For runny batters or just for a quick fix, cut an oversized piece of parchment paper, run it under the tap in the sink, then shake off the excess water and scrunch it up into a ball. When you open it out again, it will be creased and a lot more malleable. Press it into your tin, getting into the corners and making sure there is enough excess coming over the top edges. You can then pour in your more liquid batters, safe in the knowledge you have a watertight tin.

SNIP METHOD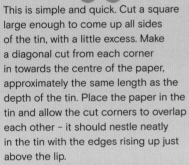
This is simple and quick. Cut a square large enough to come up all sides of the tin, with a little excess. Make a diagonal cut from each corner in towards the centre of the paper, approximately the same length as the depth of the tin. Place the paper in the tin and allow the cut corners to overlap each other – it should nestle neatly in the tin with the edges rising up just above the lip.

DISC METHOD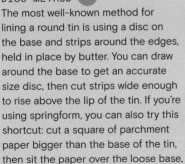
The most well-known method for lining a round tin is using a disc on the base and strips around the edges, held in place by butter. You can draw around the base to get an accurate size disc, then cut strips wide enough to rise above the lip of the tin. If you're using springform, you can also try this shortcut: cut a square of parchment paper bigger than the base of the tin, then sit the paper over the loose base,

press the collar into place and clamp the spring closed. This will create a lined base without the cutting, drawing or buttering. You'll still have to line the edges with strips – we haven't found a hack for that one yet.

CARTOUCHE
This is a useful method to learn, not only for baking but also for cooking all sorts of stews, sauces and pan-based reductions. To make a cartouche, cut a square of parchment paper slightly bigger than your round tin. Fold the paper in half diagonally to form a triangle. Repeat this step three more times, so you have a long, thin, pointy triangle. Then measure the radius by placing the tip of the triangle in the centre of your baking tin and marking where the outer edge of the paper reaches the edge of the tin. Trim the paper at this point using a pair of scissors. Unfold the triangle to reveal a round piece of paper to fit snugly on the base of your tin.

STRIP METHOD
Simply lay a thin strip of parchment paper along the length of the tin so it comes up the sides and over the edge. For more coverage, overlap another wide strip in the opposite direction to create a cross shape.

NO-PARCHMENT METHOD
If you've run out of parchment, or live in a paperless household, you can always go back to basics: butter up your tin and dust it liberally with flour or cocoa powder. This method is good for tins with a non-stick coating but it certainly isn't foolproof, and the excess parchment can't be used to lift your bakes from the tin.

OTHER EQUIPMENT

We think that the simplest way almost always makes the experience the best. Fewer gadgets means more counter and cupboard space, less money being splashed out and a more hands-on baking experience. Obviously, we're aware that some folks enjoy the shiny kitchen toys and see that as half the fun, but for us, we'd like to feel the utensils in the clutch of our floury hands, bash some nuts with a rolling pin and beat the butter until our arms pump with lactic acid. Feeling the burn and enjoying the physical side of baking helps us disconnect from the modern world and get back to using our hands. The following are the pieces of equipment that we feel are the essentials, plus a few added luxuries, if you're into the fancier things in life.

GRATER

A good grater will allow you to get the prime oily zest from your citrus fruit without the bitter pith. Box graters are useful as they have a few different grades of coarseness, plus they help to contain the zest and oils in a neat pile. Microplanes are more effective and can be used for grating hard cheese, ginger, chocolate and even garlic or chillies, so they're a great all-round investment.

MIXER

A stand mixer is a must for some people, but for us it's a bit of a luxury. We tend to mix by hand and generally find this to be a more enjoyable way to bake. However, stand mixers do offer consistent textures, a faster route to stiff peaks and are less hard work on the arms. A handheld electric whisk is a good halfway house, giving you the flexibility and versatility of a stand mixer but for less money, and without the need for counter space. You can also use a stick blender with a whisk attachment for even more ease of use.

OVEN

The most important appliance you need when it comes to baking. We've used all manner of ovens – deck, convection and gas – and we've even baked cakes on a campfire. Apparently some people make cakes in the microwave, but we're more about the traditional methods. An oven is just a source of heat and we're sure you can use the most basic one to make delicious cakes.

All the recipes in this book are written for fan-assisted electric ovens, with cakes baked on the middle shelf and a recommended turn halfway through. Every oven has a personality and nobody knows their oven quite like you. You're the best person to identify where the hot spots are, if it runs a few degrees hotter than normal or if your timer is out of whack.

Sometimes you'll have a cake that looks a little pale on top and you can always use the grill to get that added bit of caramelization to give it a healthy glow. When it's just you and your oven in the kitchen, you should be able to work the quirks out together, without things getting too heated.

OVEN THERMOMETER

Maybe the most boring bit of kit you'll ever buy, but it's really handy for getting to know your oven, especially if the thermostat isn't giving you the true visuals on what's happening inside this mythical beast. Ovens tend to have a mind of their own, and this is a good start towards getting to know yours a little better. If you have one of those probe thermometers on the end of a long metal wire, they can be used to get an accurate reading of your oven temperature, as well as perfecting your roast chicken or joint of beef, so they're not a complete waste of money.

SCALES

We recommend always going digital. They're more accurate and are usually a little more streamlined than mechanical scales, so less cupboard space is needed. If you go battery-powered, make sure to have backup batteries as you don't want to run out of power mid-weigh. Always remember to tare (zero) your scales between ingredients. You can check that they are calibrated occasionally by placing something you know the weight of on the scales.

SILICONE PARCHMENT PAPER

This stuff makes light work of getting out of sticky situations and we recommend buying this over non-siliconized paper if you can find it. The extra layer of non-stick means your cake will rarely get stuck to the paper, and saves you having to grease traditional parchment paper. It's a little slippery to work with, which makes it harder to draw on or fold, but just using a pencil rather than a pen should fix this.

SPATULA

We really want to show our appreciation for the humble spatula. They cost next to nothing, and they allow you to gently fold a cake mix or scrape down the side of your bowl during mixing, then empty the contents of the bowl into your tin, all without a scrap of wastage. The cleaner you can get the bowl, the easier the washing up, and it helps prevent your sink from getting blocked up with cake mix. We can't bang the drum loud enough for this simple bit of kit.

INGREDIENTS

At the Exploding Bakery, we believe it's important to use organic, seasonal and, most importantly, local ingredients where you can. But in reality, pretty much everyone has succumbed to the lure of year-round strawberries and supermarket prices. That's why we're happy to champion tinned or frozen fruit as a compromise. They might lack in freshness and flavour, but a tin of peaches from the far reaches of your cupboard can always be used to make a knockout cobbler, crumble or fill a hearty flapjack. Here's a list of some of the core ingredients we use in the book, and why we've chosen them. There are also some tips on what you can do if they're not available to you.

BUTTER

It's best to use unsalted butter, unless the recipe states otherwise, but if you only have salted butter, just leave out any salt in the recipe. A 250g (9oz) block of butter has about 1 teaspoon of salt. That said, salted butter has its advantages – the salt preserves it, meaning it can be kept out of the fridge, at room temperature, ready to be used. Don't throw away the wrapper: you can use it to grease your tins.

EGGS

All our recipes are made using medium eggs, so you'll always know that the contents of your egg weigh about 50g (1¾oz). If you start going rogue and buying the large, then next week the medium, you'll most likely have to get the calculator out and you could end up over-egging your pudding.

The fresher the egg, the more stable the bake. Using room temperature eggs will help to create a smooth batter. If the eggs are cold, the fats will firm up, which can make your mixture go lumpy.

GLUTEN FREE

For those who can't stomach gluten, it's not all doom and gloom. We've found Doves Farm Freee flour to be pretty good as a straight swap for wheat flour. It does come with a change in texture, but the results are still super tasty and worth the compromise. You can also add a little polenta or ground almonds for some extra texture and flavour. Some cakes even benefit from being completely wheat free, especially when you use ground nut flours. You can try swapping out the flour in our recipes using these techniques – you never know, they might taste even better.

GROUND ALMONDS

In all the recipes, we refer to 'ground almonds' (also known as almond flour), which are finely ground blanched almonds. 'Almond meal' is more coarsely ground, with the skins left on, which add small brown flecks.

We've been baking with almonds for years. They add so much texture and flavour that you simply don't get from conventional wheat flours. What they won't bring to the party is gluten, so we often blend them with a little flour to help hold things together. A nut free alternative is polenta or semolina.

OIL

Using oil is a great way to get some alternative flavours into your baking, like the pepperiness of a good olive or the grassy notes from a cold-pressed rapeseed (canola) oil. Replacing butter with oil can also make your cake dairy free. If you just want a dairy free substitute without any extra flavour, use a neutral oil like sunflower. We avoid all palm oil in our bakery, partly because margarine does not taste good and, more importantly, because any claims on sustainability are debatable.

SELF-RAISING FLOUR

This is just plain (all-purpose) flour with added raising agents. We've used self-raising flour where we can, so you don't have to faff around with bicarbonate of soda (baking soda) or baking powder. If you don't have any, just add about 1 teaspoon baking powder to 100g (3½oz) plain flour and mix thoroughly to ensure you get an even bake.

SUGAR

We're big advocates of using one type of ingredient where we can. That's why we've mainly stuck to caster (superfine) sugar. If you don't have caster sugar to hand, granulated is just a coarser caster sugar, so will still do the trick. Icing (confectioners') sugar is just more finely ground caster sugar and will also work.

Brown sugars such as muscovado and soft light brown sugar are different. They are less refined and give a slightly more caramelized flavour, along with a darker bake. If your recipe calls for one of these, the addition of some black treacle can create this if you don't have the right type of sugar to hand.

To make light brown sugar, add a tablespoon of dark treacle or molasses to 200g (7oz) of caster sugar. To make dark muscovado sugar, add 2 tablespoons of black treacle and mix with a fork in a bowl.

ULTRA-PROCESSED

Avoiding ultra-processed foods is in the zeitgeist and we think it's about time. Understanding what's in our food and where it comes from is key to our future, to create a more stable food system and protect our health. In a nutshell, ultra-processed foods are made using processes that are not associated with home cooking.

Avoiding additives, preservatives, colourants and artificial sweeteners is key to making sure we have a good starting point from which to build our recipes. Just don't get confused about the term 'processed' because cooking is a form of processing, and so is milling flour, churning butter and refining sugar. The harmful part happens when these ingredients are processed on an industrial scale, often as a cost-cutting exercise or to stabilize them for a longer shelf-life.

DAIRY

We've used various types of dairy and each contributes something different, so unfortunately you can't just chop and change due to varying water, fat and acidity levels.

Yogurt and sour cream add moisture and tanginess, enhancing the tenderness of the cake's crumb, while also adding a slight acidity that can make it rise better. Crème fraîche, which is similar to sour cream but richer and less tangy, adds a subtle creaminess and a luxurious texture.

Mascarpone, the Ferrari of cream cheese – though milder and creamier – is perfect for delicate desserts like our tiramisu (see page 107). Double (heavy) cream adds a luxurious, smooth texture and richness to whipped toppings and ganaches, contributing to a velvety mouthfeel.

When you're deciding which brand or variety of dairy to buy for your bakes, it's always a good idea to check the water and fat contents and make a side by side comparison, as things like cream cheese and yogurt can differ a lot from one another, meaning you have a little more control over whether to add richness or moisture.

We've put together some easy wins to guide you in the kitchen and make your baking dreams even more dreamy. We're big advocates of doing the simple things and making life in the kitchen as easy as possible. These useful tips are some of the lessons we've learned. They're not faddy hacks or overcomplicated tricks, just useful techniques and little wins to keep you on top of your game.

ZESTING AND JUICING

It's always best to zest your fruit before cutting it. Even if you're not planning on using the zest for that particular bake, you can freeze it for use another time.

If you have a particularly stubborn and pithy lemon or lime, you can roll it under your palm on the work surface, applying some weight to help get the juices flowing. Another little trick to revive an older lemon is to cut it in half and pop it in the microwave for a few seconds – the heat will enable you to get a few more precious drops of juice.

COOLING

Unless you're serving up a hot dessert, it's best to keep your cool and allow your cake to come down to room temperature before attempting to remove it from the tin. If you're in a rush or can't wait to taste the fruits of your labour, putting the hot bake in the freezer for a short while will help you cut that corner.

CUTTING

Sometimes you'll want to serve up a slice that's all clean lines and straight edges – maybe you've got an architect over for dessert who you want to impress. To achieve this, you'll benefit from a chilled cake and a hot knife. The best way to heat your knife is in hot water. Just make sure it's sharp and you wipe the blade between cuts. Once you've carved your geometric masterpiece, leave it to come back up to room temperature to allow the flavours to shine.

FREEZING

Don't be shy about using the freezer. It's a great way not only to preserve your bakes but also to help steady the structures for when you need to spread some buttercream over a dainty sponge or set a runny icing in a hurry. It's good to be aware that some ingredients, like nuts, may lose their crunch, and fresh fruit will lose any lust for life it once had after being frozen.

STERILIZING

To sterilize your jam jars, preheat your oven to 160°C fan/320°F/Gas 4. Give your jars a good wash in some hot, soapy water, then rinse them and place them upside down on a clean baking tray (sheet pan). Do not dry them. Place the tray in the oven for 15 minutes, then remove the jars from the oven and they are ready to use!

A cheat's version of sterilizing is to pour some boiling water in the jar and let it sit for a minute before tipping it away. This method is not as solid as canning, but it will help preserve things. Not to worry: you can use up your jam in the recipes on page 81, 91 or 118.

EASY WINS

READ THE RECIPE

Of course you're going to read it, but how about reading the entire recipe before you start anything. This will enable you to plan out the whole process, understand the time needed and know which equipment and ingredients to have ready. Essentially it's about making sure you don't get your meringues in a twist.

ROLLING PIN

If you ever find yourself up shortcrust creek without a rolling pin, a straight-edged wine bottle will get you out of trouble. Don't bash your nuts with this one though.

TOOTHPICK TEST

Obviously, a skewer or knife will do the trick too, but a toothpick is the better choice for checking whether your cake is cooked as it will make a less noticeable hole in the centre of your cake. You can also keep it in your mouth, looking slick while you wait to test. If you are making a cake that requires a swirling of jam or peanut butter, a toothpick will make light work of that too.

WEIGH AHEAD

It may create a bit more washing up, but weighing your ingredients into bowls beforehand, then putting them in the order they will be used, will help alleviate stress so you can enjoy the process. This includes peeling and dicing fruit, zesting and juicing. Even removing the lid from a tub of cream before you start is better than trying to get the grip needed with buttery fingers. And, that way, you're less likely to miss out ingredients, too.

VEGAN

We want to bang the vegan drum and commend anyone who has chosen to adopt this diet for the sake of animal welfare and for our planet. We feel with some creativity most recipes can be transformed into vegan alternatives. Swapping butter for oil normally works as a straight swap, with some binding and raising agents to replace the egg. These include ingredients like ground flaxseed, or apple or banana purée. Luckily the vegan community is a sharing one, and there's a lot of useful information out there to help make your bakes plant-based.

Look out for the VE and GF symbols to easily spot recipes that are suitable for these dietary requirements.

REAL CAKE, REAL REAL QUICK

These recipes are made for the busy folks - those people whose calendars usually mean that baking a cake is never an option. It's for those who forget the birthday cake they said they'd collect on their way home and for the time-poor cake lovers who want fresh bakes instead of supermarket fakes. In this chapter, we will shatter the myth that delicious cakes require endless hours of prep, complicated steps and tricky-to-source ingredients. Here are a bunch of recipes that can be whizzed up in a flash and flung in the oven, so you can get on with living your best life. You'll still need to factor in oven baking times, as you can't cut corners with them, but all these recipes can be oven-ready within 30 minutes. Sometimes good things can come to those who can't wait.

NO-WEIGH BLUEBERRY CAKE

In a world of information overload, it's nice to be able to strip things back and not have to think too much. This is an adaptation of a classic French recipe so simple it's taught in schools. You use just one pot to measure pretty much all the ingredients, which means no scales or jugs – just fill up, mix and bake. Most often, baking is an exact science, but here it's more of an improvised experiment, classroom-style. You can even use the pot for a hat afterwards, if you're feeling jazzy.

We've used a 150ml (5fl oz) pot of cream as the one pot to rule them all, so a similar size is recommended if you can find it.

1 x 150ml (5fl oz) pot of sour cream
2 pots of caster (superfine) sugar
3 pots of self-raising flour
1 teaspoon baking powder
1 pot of neutral oil
3 eggs
1 teaspoon vanilla paste
2 pots of blueberries
    (200–300g/7–10½oz),
    plus extra for scattering

icing (confectioners') sugar, for
    dusting

Preheat the oven to 160°C fan/320°F/Gas 4 and line your 20cm (8in) round tin using the scrunch-up method (see page 11).

To make the cake, put all the ingredients except the blueberries in a large mixing bowl and whisk them together slowly. An electric whisk makes this job much easier if you have one. As the mixture comes together, you can start to whisk a little more vigorously until well combined. Finally, fold in your blueberries.

Pour into your lined tin and bake for 70 minutes, or until a toothpick inserted comes out clean. The cake is ready when it is just set in the middle and the blueberries are caramelized and starting to burst.

Allow the cake to cool fully, then remove from the tin. Finish with a generous blizzard of icing sugar, fresh blueberries and some yogurt or cream on the side, if you like.

NOTE: This recipe will work using frozen blueberries, though you will need to bake the cake for 5-10 minutes longer, making sure to check it regularly.

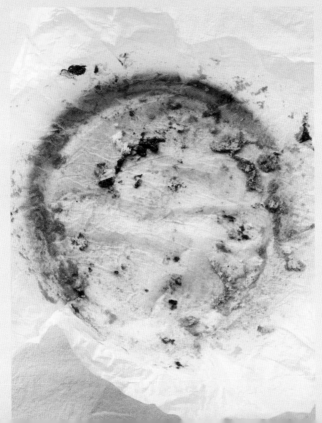

NO-WEIGH LEMON CAKE

The idea of mayonnaise in a cake may turn some people's stomachs, but this ingredient is made from emulsified fat and egg. That's half the ingredients you need to make a cake, so all you need to do is mix in sugar, flour and some flavours. We've come up with a no-weigh method too, using just a standard 250ml (9fl oz) mayonnaise jar, streamlining cake-making to show you the proof of the pudding is in the eating.

1 x 250ml (9fl oz) jar of mayonnaise
1 jar of caster (superfine) sugar
2 jars of self-raising flour
2 lemons
a pinch of salt

Preheat the oven to 180°C fan/350°F/Gas 6 and line your 20cm (8in) square tin using the snip method (see page 11).

Empty the jar of mayonnaise into a mixing bowl and scrape out as much as you can with a spatula. Fill the jar with sugar and add to the mixing bowl, then add two jarfuls of self-raising flour. Do not mix.

Finely zest the lemons into the mixing bowl. Squeeze the juice into the same mayonnaise jar, using a sieve to catch any pips. Top up the lemon juice with water until the jar is about halfway full, then pour the lemon juice and water blend into the mixing bowl, along with a pinch of salt.

Whisk all the ingredients together until you have a smooth batter with no lumps. Pour the mixture into the lined tin and bake for 1 hour, or until a toothpick inserted comes out clean and the top has become golden brown. Allow the cake to cool fully before removing from the tin.

NOTE: This cake, while perfectly delicious, might feel a bit on the simple side. You can add some jazz in the form of vanilla, a splash of rose water or some flaked almonds on top and serve with crème fraîche or whipped cream. But give this recipe a try first: we feel it's a great example of cake not needing to be complicated.

BROWN BUTTER, LEMON & RASPBERRY CAKE

Sometimes you just have to take your hat off to a classic flavour combination. Raspberry and lemon are a union that produce a crescendo of acidic fruitiness. We've added brown butter to bring some extra nuttiness to the table and create a mellow balance. You can substitute the raspberries for blueberries and lemon for orange zest with an orange curd to give this your own twist.

TO MAKE THE CAKE

100g (3½oz) butter
180g (6¼oz) caster (superfine) sugar
150g (5½oz) self-raising flour
¼ teaspoon salt
3 eggs
100ml (3½fl oz) sour cream
finely grated zest of 1 lemon
100g (3½oz) raspberries

TO MAKE THE TOPPING

250g (9oz) mascarpone
½ jar of lemon curd (about 160g/5½oz), or see page 139 for homemade
50g (1¾oz) raspberries

Preheat the oven to 160°C fan/320°F/Gas 4 and line your 20cm (8in) round tin (see page 11).

Start by browning the butter. Place the butter in a pan over a low heat and cook for about 10 minutes whilst stirring gently. It will start to form brown bits as it caramelizes. Let it foam away until it is deep, caramel brown in colour and starts to smell delicious and nutty, then immediately remove from the heat and place into a bowl. Set aside and leave to cool for 5 minutes.

Next, mix the sugar, flour and salt together in a stand mixer or large mixing bowl, then pour in the brown butter, including any brown solids, and mix well until you have an even, sandy texture. Add the eggs, sour cream and lemon zest and combine until smooth. Finally, lightly crush the fresh raspberries in your hands and add to the mixture, then fold everything together.

Scrape the batter into your tin and bake for 40 minutes, until the top becomes golden brown and a toothpick inserted into the middle of the cake comes out clean.

To make the topping, whisk together the mascarpone and lemon curd until thick and creamy. When the cake is fully cooled, remove from the tin and spread over the mascarpone icing, then decorate with more raspberries.

RUM & RAISIN BANANA CAKE

Everyone knows about banana purgatory. There's one in every kitchen. The apples and oranges don't want to hang out and the fruit flies are starting to circle. But salvation is here in recipe form, where you can peacefully lay your ripe old friends to rest. While there seem to be endless banana bread iterations out there, this one is a little different, with a boozy twist bringing the heady aromas of flambé banana to your cake. The caramel icing is a next-level addition, which will elevate any banana bread recipe, if you already have a favourite.

TO MAKE THE CAKE
100g (3½oz) raisins
2 tablespoons dark rum
120g (4¼oz) butter
2–3 ripe bananas (about 250g/9oz peeled weight)
150g (5½oz) soft light brown sugar
3 eggs
100ml (3½fl oz) sour cream
250g (9oz) self-raising flour
1 teaspoon baking powder
½ teaspoon salt

TO MAKE THE CARAMEL
100g (3½oz) soft light brown sugar
100ml (3½fl oz) sour cream
2 tablespoons dark rum
1 teaspoon vanilla paste

If you have time, soak your raisins in the rum for a few hours or overnight; if not, then for as long as possible.

Preheat the oven to 180°C fan/350°F/Gas 6 and line your 2lb (900g) loaf tin using the scrunch-up method (see page 11).

Place the butter in a pan over a low heat and cook for about 10 minutes whilst stirring gently. It will start to form brown specks as it caramelizes. Let it foam away until it is chestnut-brown in colour and starts to smell delicious and nutty, then remove from the heat and set aside to cool a little.

Mash the bananas with the sugar in a mixing bowl until they form a paste, then beat in the eggs and sour cream to form an emulsion. Add your rum-soaked raisins and melted brown butter (including any solids that have congregated at the bottom of the pan) and give a further mix until combined. Sift in the flour, baking powder and salt and combine to make a smooth, consistent batter.

Scrape the batter into your lined loaf tin and bake for 50–60 minutes, or until a toothpick inserted comes out clean and the cake is brown on top.

While the cake is cooking, make the caramel. Place the sugar and 50ml (1¾fl oz) of water in a saucepan over a medium heat and cook until the sugar dissolves, then leave to simmer for about 5 minutes. Add the sour cream, rum and vanilla and whisk continuously to make a runny beige caramel, letting it bubble up in the pan as you whisk. Turn the heat down, stop whisking and cook for a further 15 minutes so it becomes a bit darker in colour, then remove from the heat. It will thicken as it cools.

Allow the cake to cool fully, then remove from the tin and pour over the rum caramel, allowing it to drizzle down the sides of the cake a little. Slice and serve. Great with a little more sour cream if there's some spare.

NOTE: You could decorate with some broken-up banana chips, which will add a bit of texture too.

AMARETTI CAKE

In the UK, amaretti biscuits were deemed to be the height of sophistication back in the 90s. Serving them with real coffee in a cafetière really sealed the deal on arriving to middleclassdom. These biscuits have been kicking around Italy for hundreds of years and usually come in two styles: secchi, which are the brittle, dry ones, and morbidi, which are the softer, chewier ones. This recipe gives you both options. Serve a delicate slice alongside an espresso to really set you apart from the Lotus biscuit brigade.

120g (4¼oz) egg whites (from about 4 eggs)
200g (7oz) caster (superfine) sugar
50g (1¾oz) runny honey
finely grated zest of 1 lemon
finely grated zest of 1 orange
¼ teaspoon salt
½ teaspoon orange blossom water or orange extract
400g (14oz) ground almonds

icing (confectioners') sugar, for dusting

Preheat the oven to 160°C fan/320°F/Gas 4 and line your 2lb (900g) loaf tin using the scrunch-up method (see page 11).

Whisk the egg whites and sugar in a mixing bowl until you create a white emulsion and peaks just start to form when you lift the whisk out. A stand mixer or electric whisk will make this easier, but you can do it by hand if you have forearms like Rocky Balboa. Warm the honey in a saucepan or in the microwave until it starts to bubble, then slowly pour the hot honey into the bowl with the eggs, whisking until well combined.

Add the lemon and orange zest, salt and orange blossom water and mix together. Then add the ground almonds and mix to form a runny, pourable dough. Pour the mixture into your tin and bake for 45–50 minutes until it turns deep beige. If it starts to get too dark, cover it with foil.

The cake will firm up as it cools, but it will remain soft and chewy in the middle. For chewy, marzipan-style biscotti, simply dust with icing sugar, slice thinly and serve. Alternatively, place your slices on a baking tray (sheet pan) and send them back to the oven for 10 minutes at 150°C fan/300°F/Gas 3½ to turn them into crunchier biscotti, as photographed.

NOTE: Adding some flaked almonds on top, before baking, will make this look complete in the world of the amaretti biscuit.

GRAPE RICOTTA LOAF

The peppery notes of a good olive oil really shine through in this cake. It has an almost frangipane-like texture, which cradles the fruit on top of the cake. It's a versatile recipe, so using red grapes will add a sweetness and colourful contrast, while sharp white grapes bring zingy acidity. If you don't have polenta, you can simply use a plain (all-purpose) flour alternative in its place.

TO MAKE THE TOPPING
juice of 1 zested lemon (see below)
200g (7oz) seedless grapes (white, black or mixed is fine)
3 tablespoons caster (superfine) sugar
1 tablespoon fennel seeds

TO MAKE THE CAKE
150g (5½oz) caster (superfine) sugar
150g (5½oz) ricotta
3 eggs
100ml (3½fl oz) extra virgin olive oil
zest of 1 lemon
100g (3½oz) ground almonds
75g (2½oz) polenta
2 teaspoons baking powder
1 teaspoon salt

icing (confectioners') sugar, for dusting (optional)

Preheat the oven to 170°C fan/340°F/Gas 5 and line your 2lb (900g) loaf tin using the snip method (see page 11).

To make the topping, squeeze the juice of the zested lemon into a medium-sized bowl, reserving the zest for the cake. Slice your grapes into random sizes and shapes and place half in the bowl, along with the sugar. Roughly crush your fennel seeds in a pestle and mortar, or chop with a knife, then add these to the bowl too.

To make the cake batter, whisk the sugar and ricotta together in a large bowl until smooth, then add the eggs and oil and combine. An electric whisk makes this job much easier if you have one. Next, add the lemon zest, ground almonds and polenta. Sift in the baking powder and salt and mix until smooth. Finally, gently fold in the remaining grapes, then decant the mix into your loaf tin.

Scatter the now macerated grapes and any remaining lemon juice over the top. Bake in the oven for 50-55 minutes until the cake has risen, the grapes are looking jammy and a toothpick inserted comes out clean.

Leave the cake to cool before taking out of the tin and giving it a dusting of icing sugar, if you want some contrast.

GRAPEFRUIT DRIZZLE LOAF

The sunny grapefruit takes centre stage in this recipe. It's our take on the lemon drizzle, with a little more colour and vibrancy. Grapefruit is bold but under-appreciated, particularly the red and ruby varieties. Here, it adds a wink of distinction that puts lemon drizzle in the shade.

TO MAKE THE CAKE
200g (7oz) soft butter
200g (7oz) caster (superfine) sugar
4 eggs
200g (7oz) self-raising flour
1 teaspoon baking powder
¼ teaspoon salt
1 teaspoon vanilla paste
finely grated zest of ½ grapefruit

TO MAKE THE TOPPING
100g (3½oz) caster (superfine)
  sugar
juice of 1 grapefruit (about
  100ml/3½fl oz)

yogurt or crème fraîche, to serve
  (optional)

Preheat the oven to 180°C fan/350°F/Gas 6 and line your 2lb (900g) loaf tin (see page 11).

To make the cake, beat together the butter and sugar until pale and fluffy. Then add the eggs, one at a time, and scrape down the sides of the bowl between each mix. Sift in your flour, baking powder and salt and fold in to form a smooth batter. Finally, add the vanilla and grapefruit zest and give a last gentle mix before pouring into your loaf tin.

Bake for 35–40 minutes until the top of the cake becomes golden brown and a toothpick inserted into the middle comes out clean.

While the cake is cooking, make the drizzle topping. Put the sugar in a bowl and add the grapefruit juice. Don't worry if any pulp gets in – it adds to the aesthetic – but be sure to catch any seeds. Mix the juice and sugar to form a granular paste, then tip this over the top of the hot cake whilst it's still in the tin. Leave the juice to soak into the cake.

Allow the cake to cool, then remove from the tin, slice and serve with a hefty dollop of yogurt or crème fraîche, if you like.

NOTE: For some added sophistication, add a couple of shots of gin to your drizzle to bring some grown-up flavours to the party.

CARAWAY SEED CAKE

Just as it does in savoury breads, the earthy, liquorice flavour of caraway can elevate sweet bakes and has been traditionally used in British seed cakes since the Victorian times. This is a cake that brings an echo of a bygone era, a little slice of history when afternoon tea was a grand affair and cakes were the centrepiece of conversation, although every day at the Exploding Bakery is like that still.

200g (7oz) caster (superfine) sugar
4 eggs
150ml (5fl oz) olive oil or neutral oil
300g (10½oz) ground almonds
1 tablespoon caraway seeds
1 teaspoon baking powder
1 teaspoon vanilla paste
¼ teaspoon salt

runny honey, for drizzling
Greek yogurt, to serve

Preheat the oven to 170°C fan/340°F/Gas 5 and line your 2lb (900g) loaf tin (see page 11).

Beat the sugar and eggs together in a mixing bowl until they become frothy. Slowly pour in the oil while mixing continuously until you have a smooth and glossy batter. Add the almonds, caraway seeds, baking powder, vanilla and salt and mix until fully combined.

Pour the mixture into your loaf tin and bake for 65–75 minutes, or until golden brown on top and a toothpick inserted comes out clean. If the cake is is getting too dark on top but isn't cooked through, cover with foil and bake for a little longer. Remove from the oven and leave to cool, then remove from the tin and slice. Delicious served with a drizzle of honey and a dollop of yogurt.

NOTES: Try blitzing up some other nuts to use in place of some of the ground almonds. Hazelnuts, pistachio or cashews will bring a different nutty dimension.

To make the caraway flavour a little more pronounced, lightly toast the seeds, then grind them up with a pestle and mortar before adding to the batter. You can elevate the aromatics even further with a little orange zest or a splash of rose water.

STORE CUPBOARD HEROES

It's time to face your hoarding fears, get up on your tiptoes and peer into the dark forgotten corners of your pantry. This is all about digging out those dusty old jars and reconnecting with that bag of sultanas you've been avoiding eye contact with for months. Get ready to clear your cupboards, boost your baking repertoire, and relish the unexpected heroes that have been hiding in plain sight. This isn't just an exercise in decluttering, it's a baking revolution from the back of your cupboard.

BERRY CITRUS CAKE

Our bakery was given the challenge to make something for our wholesale customers that added a splash of colour to their counters. After weeks of testing various icings and using different brightly coloured fruits, this was the vibrant result. This is a recipe you can make using that old store cupboard staple and all-round favourite: jam. We found that the sharp acidity and herbaceous flavour of blackcurrant works best if you happen to have any, but feel free to try any other berry preserves.

TO MAKE THE CAKE
240ml (8fl oz) soya milk
1 teaspoon white wine vinegar
65g (2¼oz) soft light brown sugar
65g (2¼oz) caster (superfine)
    sugar
finely grated zest of 1 lemon
finely grated zest of 1 orange
65ml (2¼fl oz) rapeseed (canola)
    oil
60g (2¼oz) dairy-free yogurt (we
    used plain soya yogurt)
240g (8½oz) self-raising flour
1 teaspoon baking powder
½ teaspoon bicarbonate of soda
    (baking soda)
115g (4oz) blackcurrant preserve (or
    a good-quality blackcurrant jam)

TO MAKE THE BUTTERCREAM
75g (2½oz) vegan butter
    (preferably vegan block butter,
    not spreadable)
150g (5½oz) icing (confectioners')
    sugar, sifted
2 teaspoons lemon juice
1½ tablespoons blackcurrant
    preserve

edible flower petals, for sprinkling
    (if you can get hold of them); if
    not, a fresh berry on each slice
    will look good

Preheat your oven to 170°C fan/340°F/Gas 5 and line a 20cm (8in) square tin (see page 11).

To make the cake, pour the soya milk into a small mixing bowl and add the white wine vinegar. Stir well, then leave to thicken for a few minutes.

Next, put the sugars, lemon zest, orange zest, oil, yogurt and the milk-vinegar mixture in a large mixing bowl. Give everything a good stir, making sure there are no lumps of sugar remaining.

Sift the self-raising flour, baking powder and bicarbonate of soda into the wet ingredients and mix until the flour has absorbed the wet ingredients. Scrape the sides and bottom of the bowl with a spatula, then give everything one last mix until you achieve a smooth batter, being careful not to overmix.

Pour the batter into your prepared tin. Spoon small dollops of the blackcurrant preserve on top of the cake batter, then swirl it through the batter using a skewer to create a 'marble' effect.

Bake for 30 minutes or until a toothpick inserted comes out clean and the cake springs back when pressed. Leave it to cool for 10 minutes, then remove from the tin and allow it to cool completely.

Whilst the cake is cooling, make the icing. Place the butter into a mixing bowl and beat until soft. Add the icing sugar, lemon juice and blackcurrant preserve and beat until you have a smooth, colourful icing, scraping down the sides if necessary. If your icing is too runny, you can add a little more icing sugar. If it is too thick, you can loosen it with some more blackcurrant preserve.

Once the cake is cool, top with your prepared icing, spreading it evenly to the edges. Finish with a light dusting of edible flower petals for a bit of colour, if you have them, or berries.

CHOCOLATE & MARMALADE CAKE

For those unfamiliar, a jaffa cake is a flat sponge topped with a little bit of orange jelly and covered in chocolate, and it is pretty much the go-to indulgence for this particular flavour combo. With good reason too – the flavour balance is just right – so we've used that as a yardstick for this recipe. The combination of chocolate and orange with the subtle grassiness of olive oil is an absolute winner. You don't have to use the world's best olive oil and this recipe is especially good for using up that old jar of marmalade you've had kicking around for years.

TO MAKE THE CAKE

100g (3½oz) caster (superfine)
  sugar
3 eggs
180ml (6fl oz) extra virgin olive oil
180g (6¼oz) self-raising flour
½ teaspoon baking powder
¼ teaspoon fine salt
100g (3½oz) dark chocolate drops
40g (1½oz) ground almonds
finely grated zest and juice of
  1 orange

TO MAKE THE TOPPING

100g (3½oz) fine-cut marmalade
  (see page 137 for homemade)
200g (7oz) dark chocolate, broken
  into pieces

Preheat the oven to 160°C fan/320°F/Gas 4 and line your 20cm (8in) round tin using the strip method (see page 11).

To make the cake, beat the sugar and eggs together by hand in a large mixing bowl, until they become light and frothy. Whilst mixing, slowly pour in the olive oil so it emulsifies.

Sift in the flour, baking powder and salt and gently fold together. Add the chocolate, ground almonds and the zest and juice of an orange and give one last fold.

Pour the mixture into your tin and bake for 40–45 minutes, or until golden and a toothpick inserted comes out clean. Leave the cake to cool almost completely. It will have domed slightly – slice across the top to remove the dome and nibble on it while you bake. Spread the marmalade evenly over the flat area of the cake.

Melt the chocolate in a heatproof bowl over a pan of barely simmering water, ensuring the bowl doesn't touch the water. Once melted, leave it to cool for around 5 minutes, then pour on top of the marmalade, allowing the chocolate to run down the sides of the cake. You might need to help it to the edges with a spatula depending on how runny or thick it is.

Now leave the chocolate to set for 40 minutes. To create the classic jaffa cake grid on the top, press a knife lightly and gently into the chocolate.

Once completely set, warm a sharp knife with hot water to get a clean cut through the cake.

NOTES: If you can't get hold of dark chocolate drops, breaking up a bar will do the trick.

We use a well set marmalade with a high fruit content – look for one with around 40% fruit.

MAPLE & PECAN FRIAND

After pancake day, that bottle of maple syrup can really linger in your cupboard like a guest who's outstayed their welcome. Here's a way to use it up, utilizing that deep, nutty flavour and matching it perfectly with its best mate, the pecan. And pull out your ground almonds from the back of the cupboard – they bring bags of flavour and texture to this floaty, moist sponge. Ideally, you'd mix this cake the day before it's baked. The batter, similar to pancakes and madeleines, is better after being in the fridge for at least a few hours. The icing can be made in advance too.

TO MAKE THE CAKE
150g (5½oz) salted butter
240g (8½oz) egg whites (from about 7 eggs)
220g (7¾oz) icing (confectioners') sugar
100g (3½oz) plain (all-purpose) flour
1 teaspoon baking powder
80g (2¾oz) ground almonds
60ml (2fl oz) maple syrup
80g (2¾oz) pecan pieces, roughly chopped

TO MAKE THE ICING
100g (3½oz) soft salted butter
60ml (2fl oz) maple syrup
250g (9oz) icing (confectioners') sugar, sifted

6 pecan halves, to decorate
icing (confectioners') sugar, for dusting
maple syrup, for drizzling (optional)

Place the butter in a pan over a low heat and cook for about 10 minutes whilst stirring gently. It will start to form brown specks as it caramelizes. Let it foam away until it is chestnut-brown in colour and starts to smell delicious and nutty, then remove from the heat and set aside to cool very slightly.

Put the egg whites in a stand mixer or large mixing bowl and whisk until they start to thicken and become airy. If you don't have a stand mixer, an electric whisk makes this job much easier, or you can even do this by hand if you have forearms like Popeye. Sift in the icing sugar, flour and baking powder and fold everything together until combined. Add the ground almonds, melted butter, maple syrup and pecan pieces and gently mix until it becomes a glossy batter.

Put the cake batter in the fridge to chill until you're ready to use it, ideally for at least 3 hours, but it'll keep for a couple of days in the fridge.

When you're ready to bake the cake, preheat the oven to 180°C fan/ 350°F/Gas 6 and line your 20cm (8in) round tin using the scrunch-up method (see page 11).

Scrape the mixture into your prepared tin and bake in the centre of the oven for 40–45 minutes until the top of the cake becomes golden brown and a toothpick inserted comes out clean. Leave the cake to cool in the tin.

To make the icing, beat the butter in a large bowl until it is light in colour. Add the maple syrup and the icing sugar and beat until perfectly smooth. If it's too runny, add a little more icing sugar. If it's too stiff, add a little more maple syrup to loosen.

Remove the cooled cake from the tin and cover the top with the icing, spreading it evenly to the edges. If you've made the icing ahead of time, you will need to bring it to room temperature to ensure it's spreadable – you may need to whip it into shape a little.

Decorate with pecan halves, dust with icing sugar and add a final drizzle of maple syrup, if you like.

ORANGE & CARDAMOM LOAF

If you have a bag of polenta or semolina knocking around that was bought with good intentions, this is a tasty way to clear that cupboard space for your next adventurous grocery purchase. This recipe is adapted from one of our wholesale recipes, using semolina instead of polenta to give a lighter bite for those who find polenta a bit on the crunchy side. As we're a nation of avid curry makers, lots of us have the odd jar of cardamom pods kicking around too.

TO MAKE THE CAKE

180g (6¼oz) soft butter
180g (6¼oz) caster (superfine)
  sugar
finely grated zest and juice of
  1 orange
150g (5½oz) ground almonds
3 eggs
100g (3½oz) fine semolina (cream
  of wheat)
1 teaspoon baking powder
½ teaspoon ground cardamom,
  from around 15 pods (see note)

TO MAKE THE SYRUP

juice of 1 orange (about
  50ml/1¾fl oz)
50g (1¾oz) caster (superfine)
  sugar

Preheat the oven to 170°C fan/340°F/Gas 5 and line a 2lb (900g) loaf tin using the scrunch-up method (see page 11).

To make the cake, cream the butter and sugar in a stand mixer or large mixing bowl with a wooden spoon, until light and fluffy. Add the orange zest and ground almonds.

Add the eggs one at a time and mix, scraping the sides of the bowl to ensure everything is well incorporated. Add the semolina, baking powder and cardamom and give it a light mix while pouring in the orange juice.

Pour the cake batter into your loaf tin and bake for 40–45 minutes, or until a toothpick inserted comes out clean. The top should form a lovely crust and the cake will turn dark golden-brown.

While the cake is baking, make the syrup. Squeeze the juice of an orange into a saucepan and add the sugar, then place over a medium heat. Stir continuously until the sugar dissolves, then bring to a simmer to reduce the liquid slightly. Once it is syrupy, take it off the heat.

When the cake comes out of the oven, spoon the hot syrup over the top, then set aside to cool and soak up the syrupy goodness. Leave to cool a little before slicing and serving.

NOTE: To grind your own cardamom, bash the pods to break the husk and remove the seeds inside. Discard the husks and grind the seeds into a fine powder with either a spice grinder, a pestle and mortar or even a coffee grinder. If you use a coffee grinder, don't worry too much about cleaning the grinder afterwards. A little cardamom flavour will give your ground coffee a delicious twist.

CHOCOLATE STOUT CAKE

This cake is a real catch, a smooth operator of epic proportions. The stout and chocolate frosting doubles down on the flavour profile, adding to the indulgence. It's a good way to use up that unwanted four-pack of stout that a strange dinner guest brought round last year. In our bakery, this cake is known as 'black velvet', making it sound like a glam-rock band, which means you should probably serve it up wearing a sequined one-piece and blaring out a bit of T. Rex.

TO MAKE THE CAKE

190ml (6½fl oz) stout
170g (6oz) butter
50g (1¾oz) unsweetened cocoa powder
275g (9¾oz) caster (superfine) sugar
90ml (3fl oz) sour cream
3 eggs
1 teaspoon vanilla paste
190g (6¾oz) plain (all-purpose) flour
1 teaspoon bicarbonate of soda (baking soda)

TO MAKE THE TOPPING

90g (3¼oz) dark chocolate
200g (7oz) icing (confectioners') sugar
150g (5½oz) soft butter
50ml (1¾fl oz) stout

unsweetened cocoa powder, for dusting (optional)

Preheat the oven to 160°C fan/320°F/Gas 4 and line your 20cm (8in) square tin using the scrunch-up method (see page 11).

In a medium saucepan, heat the stout, butter, cocoa powder and sugar together over a medium heat, whisking until everything is melted and the sugar has dissolved.

Remove from the heat, then add the sour cream, eggs and vanilla, whisking gently until combined.

Sift your flour and bicarbonate of soda into a separate mixing bowl, then pour in the contents of the saucepan and mix gently until you have a smooth batter. Pour this into your lined tin and bake for 35 minutes, or until a toothpick inserted comes out clean, then leave to cool a little.

To make the topping, melt the chocolate in a microwave or in a heatproof bowl over a pan of barely simmering water, ensuring the bowl does not touch the water. Once melted, pour into a food processor with the remaining topping ingredients and blitz until smooth. Alternatively, you can do this by hand using a whisk. Spread over the cooled cake and dust with extra cocoa powder, if you like.

TRES LECHES MOCHA CAKE

There are plenty of ordinary store cupboard staples that you can turn into baking heroes, like that packet of instant coffee you stole from the hotel room and the tin of evaporated milk that's starting to rust a little. If you like your coffee cold, milky, full of chocolate and completely non-viscous, then this is the cake for you. In all seriousness, this cake is absolutely delicious – the coffee flavour lingers in the background while the chocolate works perfectly to complement it. The milk-soaked sponge has a special texture that is both moist and rich, while not being heavy. This is a cake that takes very little time to prepare, but looks like you've put the work in, so you can sit back and soak up the plaudits.

TO MAKE THE CAKE
100ml (3½fl oz) rapeseed (canola) or sunflower oil
200g (7oz) caster (superfine) sugar
1 teaspoon instant coffee
135ml (4½fl oz) whole milk
2 teaspoons vanilla paste
3 eggs
190g (6¾oz) plain (all-purpose) flour
1 teaspoon baking powder
20g (¾oz) unsweetened cocoa powder
½ teaspoon salt

TO MAKE THE SOAKING LIQUID
60ml (2fl oz) evaporated milk
80g (2¾oz) sweetened condensed milk
50ml (1¾fl oz) whole milk

TO MAKE THE WHIPPED CREAM
[OPTIONAL; SEE NOTE]
200ml (7fl oz) double (heavy) cream
65g (2¼oz) icing (confectioners') sugar
¼ teaspoon vanilla paste

double cream, to serve (if not making the whipped cream)
unsweetened cocoa powder, for dusting

Preheat the oven to 170°C fan/340°F/Gas 5 and line a 2lb (900g) loaf tin (see page 11).

To make the cake, put the oil, sugar, instant coffee, whole milk, vanilla paste and eggs in a mixing bowl and whisk well until all the ingredients are combined. Sift the flour, baking powder, cocoa powder and salt over the top of the wet ingredients. Using a spatula, gently fold the dry ingredients into the wet.

Pour the batter into the prepared loaf tin, spread it evenly, and bake for 45 minutes, or until lightly golden brown and it springs back when touched. Leave the cake to cool in the tin for 15–20 minutes.

Using a skewer or similar, punch holes all over the top of the cake – this will help the soaking liquid absorb properly.

In a bowl or measuring jug, whisk together the evaporated milk, condensed milk and whole milk to create the soaking liquid. Slowly pour the liquid mixture over the cake, so it can soak into the ready-made holes. Pop it into the fridge for 30–60 minutes so the cake absorbs the liquid.

While the cake is soaking, you can prepare the whipped cream topping, if using. Whisk the cream, icing sugar and vanilla paste in a stand mixer or large mixing bowl to stiff peaks. If you don't have a stand mixer, an electric whisk makes this job much easier.

Once the cake has absorbed all of the liquid, spread the whipped cream evenly over the cake, if using, or pour over as much double cream as you like. Finish with a light dusting of cocoa powder.

NOTES: This cake is great with just a little double cream on the side. But if you want to make this a proper showstopper, then you can use the soaking time to prepare a whipped cream topping.

This cake will keep for 4-5 days in the fridge. The cake also freezes well, but if you're using the whipped cream topping, add this once the cake has defrosted.

FRUIT & NUT CAKE

This fruit and nut cake is the lovechild of a traditional Christmas cake and dark chocolate, with a slight tip of the cap to the famous Cadbury's bar. We've also added a splash of booze to bring some festive cheer. If you're not that way inclined, soak the fruit in spiced tea for some added festive notes. Even without the Christmas spirit, this cake is ready to party all year round. This is a great way to use up any loitering dried fruits and nuts you might have in the cupboard – the ones we've suggested are just what we think work well. A reminder that sometimes you don't have to go full Santa-suit braces to please a Christmas crowd!

150g (5½oz) dried fruit (apricots, figs, sultanas/golden raisins, cranberries, dates)
50ml (1¾fl oz) Christmas booze (brandy, whisky, sherry, Calvados) or strong Earl Grey tea
150g (5½oz) soft butter
150g (5½oz) caster (superfine) sugar
1 teaspoon vanilla paste
3 eggs
150g (5½oz) ground almonds
¼ teaspoon salt
150g (5½oz) dark chocolate
100g (3½oz) mixed nuts (walnuts, pecans, hazelnuts, cashews)

icing (confectioners') sugar, for dusting

Chop up the dried fruit, trying to make them all about the same size – no bigger than 1cm (½in) in diameter – then soak in your booze or tea, ideally overnight or just while you prepare the rest of the cake.

Preheat the oven to 170°C fan/340°F/Gas 5 and line your 20cm (8in) round tin (see page 11).

Cream the butter and sugar in a stand mixer or a large mixing bowl using a wooden spoon, until light and fluffy. Add the vanilla and the eggs one by one, mixing well after each addition and scraping down the sides of the mixing bowl, until you have a smooth, glossy batter.

Mix in the ground almonds, salt and soaked fruit, along with any leftover soaking liquor. The mixture will split a little here, but that's ok. Smash your chocolate up into small pieces and do the same with your chosen nuts. Add both to the mix and mix to fully combine.

Scrape the batter into the tin and bake for 45–50 minutes until the top is golden brown and a toothpick inserted comes out clean. If the fruit or nuts near the top of the cake are getting too dark towards the end of baking, cover with some foil.

Leave the cake to cool completely before removing from the tin. It's even better if you make it the day before and allow the fruit to really settle into a classic fruit cake texture overnight.

Top with a generous dusting of icing sugar to serve. If you have any chocolate left over, you can grate some shavings over as well.

HUMMINGBIRD CAKE

A cake that was forged in 60s Jamaica; a showcase that was published in newspapers to spread the word and champion the vibrant and sun-soaked fruits of the island; a cake born from the unfolding global awareness of all the island has to offer and a recipe that champions the amazing flavours and produce available. Originally called the Dr Bird Cake after the island's national bird, the hummingbird, this truly has the power to heal the cake blues. It's a recipe that urges you to rummage in the cupboards for the tinned pineapple and various other packets of half-used nuts and spices.

TO MAKE THE CAKE

135ml (4½fl oz) rapeseed (canola) oil (or any flavourless oil will work)
110g (3¾oz) ripe bananas, mashed
130g (4½oz) tinned pineapple chunks, diced into small pieces
4 eggs
160g (5½oz) soft light brown sugar
190g (6¾oz) self-raising flour
1 teaspoon bicarbonate of soda (baking soda)
1 teaspoon ground cinnamon
1 teaspoon salt
2 teaspoons desiccated (dried shredded) coconut
40g (1½oz) pecans, finely chopped

TO MAKE THE ICING

200g (7oz) icing (confectioners') sugar, sifted
finely grated zest and juice of 2 limes

Caramelized Coconut Flakes (see page 135), to sprinkle (optional)

Preheat your oven to 170°C fan/340°F/Gas 5 and line a 20cm (8in) square tin using the scrunch-up method (see page 11).

To make the cake, add the oil, mashed banana, diced pineapple, eggs and brown sugar to a large mixing bowl, then mix until well combined.

Next, sift in the flour along with the bicarbonate of soda, ground cinnamon and salt, then add the desiccated coconut and diced pecans. Give everything a good mix until you have a smooth batter.

Pour the batter into the prepared tin and bake for 40 minutes, or until a toothpick inserted comes out clean and the sponge springs back when pressed. Leave to cool completely in the tin.

Whilst the cake is cooling, prepare the icing by mixing the sugar and lime zest and juice together to a smooth consistency.

Once the cake is cool, pour the icing over the top, almost as though you are 'flooding' the cake. Using a spatula, spread it evenly over the top, making sure it is fully covered. To add some extra crunch, try topping it with the coconut flakes.

SEASONAL

Being from the countryside, we like to think we're at one with nature, or at least nature adjacent. What it does mean is that we feel a strong need to make sure we're using all the seasons have to offer, learning what grows locally to us, and incorporating as much of that into our recipes as possible. This helps to stop us from falling into the supermarket trap of all-year-round, air-mile laden goodies. Growing your own, buying some dusty eggs from a rickety roadside honesty box or foraging berries from deep within some spiky bushes all bring their own rewards. And that's before you've even got into the kitchen to bake the cakes to complement the time of year.

EDEN PROJECT COURGETTE CAKE

The Eden Project is an environmental charity garden made up of giant, greenhouse-like domes, nestled in a disused claypit in Cornwall. We devised a recipe with the team for their Big Lunch event, and were tasked with making a cake using ingredients that often end up in the bin. It turns out courgettes (zucchini) are guilty of frequently dodging the cooking pot. It just so happens, courgettes are excellent at keeping things moist whilst adding a good hit of fibre. The gardeners at The Eden Project also pulled a load of rosemary out of a hat and asked us to use that too, as it grows in abundance in their geothermal plant nursery. This recipe is a force for good: promoting community, tackling food waste and getting us to think about the future of our planet.

TO MAKE THE CAKE

270g (9½oz) self-raising flour
½ teaspoon bicarbonate of soda
   (baking soda)
½ teaspoon salt
100ml (3½fl oz) rapeseed (canola)
   oil, or any neutral oil will do
225g (8oz) caster (superfine) sugar
3 eggs
finely grated zest and juice of
   1 large lemon
175g (6oz) courgette (zucchini),
   grated
½ teaspoon finely chopped fresh
   rosemary

TO MAKE THE TOPPING

130g (4½oz) icing (confectioners')
   sugar, sifted
finely grated zest and juice of
   1 large lemon

Preheat the oven to 180°C fan/350°F/Gas 6 and line a 2lb (900g) loaf tin using two strips of parchment paper (see page 11).

Sift the flour into a small mixing bowl, then add the bicarbonate of soda and salt and whisk everything together. Put the oil, sugar, eggs, lemon zest, lemon juice, grated courgette and chopped rosemary in a stand mixer or large mixing bowl and beat until everything is incorporated.

Next, add the flour, bicarbonate of soda and salt to the bowl with the courgette and mix until the flour begins to incorporate. At this point, stop and give the sides and bottom of the bowl a good scrape with a spatula. Finally, give the mix one last beat until you have a smooth cake batter, being careful not to overmix as this could result in a dense cake.

Transfer the cake batter to your prepared loaf tin and bake for 40 minutes, or until a toothpick inserted comes out mostly clean. Allow the cake to cool for 15 minutes, then carefully remove it from the tin and place on a wire rack to cool completely.

To make the lemon icing, in a small bowl mix together the icing sugar and lemon juice. You are looking for a relatively thick consistency but one that will still 'drip' down the sides of the cake when poured on top. If your icing is too thick, add more lemon juice, a teaspoon at a time, until you reach the desired consistency. Go slowly as it will very quickly become runny.

To serve, spread the lemon icing over the top of the loaf and finish with a light grating of the zest. You can either leave the icing to set or enjoy the cake straight away!

ROASTED RHUBARB & CREAM CAKE

Capturing the essence of spring with some forced rhubarb can bring some much-needed light and colour to the table after a long winter. The bright acidity paired with the vibrant fuchsia pink has been scientifically proven to warm the soul by a whole 5°C. The billowy cloud of whipped cream engulfs the sponge landscapes, allowing the bright batons of rhubarb to shine.

TO MAKE THE CAKE

220g (7¾oz) soft butter
200g (7oz) caster (superfine) sugar
4 eggs
200g (7oz) self-raising flour
1 teaspoon baking powder

TO COOK THE RHUBARB

400g (14oz) rhubarb, diced into
    2cm (¾in) batons
1 orange
50g (1¾oz) caster (superfine)
    sugar

TO MAKE THE WHIPPED CREAM

275ml (9½fl oz) double (heavy)
    cream
85g (3oz) icing (confectioners')
    sugar

Preheat the oven to 150°C fan/300°F/Gas 3½ and line your 20cm (8in) round tin (see page 11).

To make the cake, cream the butter and sugar in a stand mixer or a large mixing bowl using a wooden spoon, until light and fluffy. Add the eggs one by one, mixing well after each addition and scraping down the sides of the mixing bowl. Finally, sift in the flour and baking powder until you achieve a smooth dropping consistency. Give the bowl a last scrape to make sure all the ingredients are mixed properly.

Transfer the cake mixture to the prepared tin, smooth the top of the batter with a spatula and bake for 45 minutes or until a toothpick inserted comes out clean.

Whilst the cake is baking, prepare the rhubarb. Place the batons onto a baking tray (sheet pan) lined with parchment paper. Zest and squeeze the juice of the orange on top, then sprinkle over the sugar. Place the tray into the oven whilst your cake is baking and roast for 25–30 minutes.

Remove the cake and rhubarb from the oven, then pour the juices that have come out of the rhubarb over the sponge. Leave the cake to cool for 5 minutes, then remove from the tin and allow to fully cool.

Next, prepare the whipped cream. Pour the cream into a mixing bowl, add the icing sugar and whisk until you achieve soft peaks. An electric whisk makes this job much easier if you have one, but be careful not to over whip the cream.

Finally, assemble the cake. Add half of your roasted rhubarb to the whipped cream and mix through, then evenly spread it over the cooled sponge. Finish by piling the remaining batons of roasted rhubarb on top of the cake, then serve and enjoy!

MERINGUTAN CAKE

This feels like an autumnal celebration cake, an alternative to a Thanksgiving pumpkin pie, or something to get you in the mood for the cosy winter ahead. As the leaves start to fall from the trees, our world becomes filled with pumpkin-spiced everything. Go with the flow and embrace the warmth of chai spices and quiffs of sweet meringue. If you've ever seen an orangutan with a meringue on its head, then you'll know why we chose to call it a Meringutan Cake.

TO MAKE THE SWISS MERINGUE

2 egg whites
120g (4¼oz) caster (superfine)
  sugar

TO MAKE THE CAKE

145g (5oz) self-raising flour
2 teaspoons mixed (pumpkin pie)
  spice
1 teaspoon baking powder
½ teaspoon bicarbonate of soda
  (baking soda)
¾ teaspoon salt
160g (5½oz) caster (superfine)
  sugar
200g (7oz) tinned pumpkin purée
140ml (4¾fl oz) rapeseed (canola)
  or sunflower oil
2 eggs

Preheat the oven to 170°C fan/340°F/Gas 5 and line your 20cm (8in) square tin (see page 11).

First make the Swiss meringue. Put a pan of water on a medium heat until it reaches a gentle simmer. While it's heating up, whisk together the egg whites and sugar in a heatproof bowl. Place the bowl over the pan of barely simmering water, ensuring the bowl does not touch the water. Continue whisking until the mixture is smooth and silky with no sugar granules – you can test this by feeling it between your fingers.

Remove from the heat and continue whisking until you have stiff peaks. A stand mixer or electric whisk will make this job easier if you have one, but whisking it by hand works just as well if you have arms as strong as an orangutan. Set the meringue to one side.

To make the cake, add the dry ingredients to one bowl and the wet ingredients to another. Whisk the dry ingredients together to fully combine, then gradually add to the wet ingredients, a little bit at a time, whisking until you have a smooth batter.

Pour the batter into the prepared tin and smooth the top with a spatula. Layer the meringue on top, then, using a skewer or spoon, gently swirl the batter and meringue together to create a marbled effect.

Bake the cake for 60–70 minutes, or until a skewer comes out clean. The cake will rise, then fall back down again. This is OK and the cake will cook all the way through.

Leave the cake to cool for 20 minutes, then remove from the tin and allow to cool completely before serving.

NOTE: If you have a glut of pumpkins or squashes, you can make your own pumpkin purée. Peel and deseed your squash, then steam until tender for about 20 minutes. You can also do this in the microwave. Then mash or blend into a smooth paste. You can always pass through a sieve to avoid any lumps.

STRWBERRY LOAF

This simple sponge recipe incorporates some fruit to add a splash of colour and a bit of moisture to your sponge. It's a democratized cake, fit for a wide audience, and the charisma and good looks of the strawberries will win anyone over without the need for a politician's handshake. It certainly gets our vote.

TO MAKE THE CAKE

175g (6oz) soft butter
175g (6oz) caster (superfine) sugar
4 eggs
150g (5½oz) ground almonds
100g (3½oz) self-raising flour,
  sifted
¼ teaspoon salt
150g (5½oz) strawberries
1 teaspoon vanilla paste

TO MAKE THE ICING

50g (1¾oz) strawberries
  (2–3 strawberries)
1 tablespoon golden (corn) syrup
1 teaspoon vanilla paste
200g (7oz) icing (confectioners')
  sugar, sifted

Preheat the oven to 170°C fan/340°F/Gas 5 and line your 2lb (900g) loaf tin (see page 11).

To make the cake, cream the butter and sugar in a stand mixer or a large mixing bowl using a wooden spoon, until light and fluffy. Add the eggs one by one, mixing well after each addition and scraping down the sides of the mixing bowl.

Add the ground almonds, sift in the flour and salt, then gently fold into the mix until fully combined.

Remove the tops of the strawberries, chop them into very small chunks, then add them to the mix along with the vanilla. Give everything one final mix to make sure it's well combined, then pour into your loaf tin and bake for 60–70 minutes, rotating the tin halfway through. The cake is cooked when a toothpick inserted comes out clean. Leave to cool then remove from the tin.

To make the icing, remove the tops of your strawberries and use the back of a spoon to press the fruit through a sieve into a large bowl. Remember to scrape the bottom of the sieve to get all of the pulp as it tends to congregate there. Next, mix the golden syrup and vanilla with the strawberry pulp and sift in the icing sugar. Mix everything together to make a bright-pink icing, then pour it over the cooled loaf, allowing some to run down the sides.

NOTE: Swapping out the strawberries for blackcurrants would give this a darker blast of colour, deep-purple style.

BLUEBERRY CAKE

So, you're in need of a blueberry and lemon hit. We've all been there. Sure, you could just scoff a handful of dusty blueberries, squeeze a lemon in your mouth and continue to ignore the other ingredients begging to get involved. But this recipe satisfies your cravings and gives a whole load of attention to some other needy ingredients, who have been sitting patiently on the shelves waiting for you to pick them for your baking squadron. It also means that the moment you leave the room, the ground almonds won't talk about you behind your back.

TO MAKE THE CAKE
150g (5½oz) soft butter
150g (5½oz) caster (superfine)
 sugar
3 eggs
zest and juice of 1 lemon
150g (5½oz) ground almonds
125g (4½oz) self-raising flour
¼ teaspoon salt
150g (5½oz) blueberries, plus 50g
 (1¾oz) extra for decorating

TO MAKE THE ICING
juice of 1 lemon
200g (7oz) icing (confectioners')
 sugar

Preheat the oven to 160°C fan/320°F/Gas 4 and line your 20cm (8in) round tin (see page 11).

To make the cake, cream the butter and sugar in a stand mixer or a large mixing bowl using a wooden spoon, until light and fluffy. Add the eggs one by one, mixing well after each addition and scraping down the sides of the mixing bowl. Add the lemon zest and juice and give it a further mix, then add the ground almonds and incorporate into the mix. Sift in the flour and salt and gently fold in.

Scrape the batter into your tin and scatter the blueberries on top. If you happen to have any really big, plump blueberries, it's best to cut them in half or their weight could make them sink to the bottom of the cake.

Bake for 60–65 minutes, or until a toothpick inserted comes out clean. Leave to cool then remove from the tin.

Meanwhile, get to work on the icing. Squeeze the lemon juice into a bowl and sift in the icing sugar. Mix to form a runny icing, adding a few drops of cold water if the icing is too thick – it should be slightly runny. Pour the icing over the cooled cake and decorate with the remaining blueberries.

NOTE: This cake will certainly work with other berries, just be mindful of strawberries as they tend to hold a lot of water.

GOOSEBERRY CAKE

In our opinion, gooseberries are criminally underused, so we want to be cheerleaders for this delicious, humble berry and show the world its sharp wit and zest for life. The hint of molasses in the sponge adds a dark side to proceedings, challenging our sweet perceptions of cake and daring to be a little different. We know the season for gooseberries is quite fleeting, so if you're finding it tricky to source them, some plums, juicy black grapes or tart rhubarb will also work a treat.

175g (6oz) soft butter
125g (4½oz) caster (superfine) sugar, plus 20g (¾oz) extra for sprinkling
1 tablespoon black treacle (molasses)
1 teaspoon vanilla paste
2 eggs
100g (3½oz) ground almonds
200g (7oz) self-raising flour
1 teaspoon baking powder
¼ teaspoon sea salt
250g (9oz) gooseberries, halved

crème fraîche or Greek yogurt, to serve (optional)

Preheat the oven to 160°C fan/320°F/Gas 4 and line your 20cm (8in) square tin (see page 11).

To make the cake, cream the butter and sugar in a stand mixer or a large mixing bowl using a wooden spoon, until light and fluffy. Add the treacle, vanilla and the eggs, one by one, mixing well after each addition and scraping down the sides of the mixing bowl.

Mix in the ground almonds, then sift in the flour, baking powder and salt and gently fold together until well combined.

Scrape the batter into your prepared tin and scatter the halved gooseberries evenly over the top. Sprinkle the remaining caster sugar over the berries, place in the centre of the oven and bake for 45 minutes, or until the gooseberries are starting to look jammy and a toothpick inserted into the cake comes out clean. Leave to cool, then remove from the tin.

Serve on its own or with a big helping of crème fraîche or yogurt, if you like.

NOTE: Try topping this with the sugared almonds on page 135.

BLACKCURRANT FRIAND LOAF

What the punchy little blackcurrant lacks in stature, it makes up for with big flavour energy. The herbaceous scent transports you to the leafy outdoors, conjuring up visions of hedgerows on a glorious early summer day. In late summer and early autumn, you can use foraged blackberries, or winter raspberries will also work brilliantly. The accompanying aniseed brings a dash of ouzo or pastis to pair with the almonds, but if you want to emphasize the blackcurrant instead, you can always leave out the star anise.

TO MAKE THE CAKE
180g (6¼oz) salted butter
1 teaspoon ground star anise (or 5 whole)
150g (5½oz) egg whites (about 5 eggs)
180g (6¼oz) icing (confectioners') sugar
60g (2¼oz) self-raising flour
120g (4¼oz) ground almonds
finely grated zest of 1 lemon
150g (5½oz) frozen blackcurrants

TO MAKE THE ICING
60g (2¼oz) frozen blackcurrants, defrosted, plus extra for scattering
juice of 1 lemon
200g (7oz) icing (confectioners') sugar

Preheat the oven to 190°C fan/375°F/Gas 6–7 and line a 2lb (900g) loaf tin using the snip method (see page 11).

Place the butter in a pan over a low heat and cook for about 10 minutes whilst stirring gently. It will start to form brown specks as it caramelizes. If you are using whole star anise instead of ground, add these to the butter to infuse while it is browning. Let the butter foam away until it is chestnut-brown in colour and starts to smell delicious and nutty, then remove from the heat and set aside to cool a little, but not set.

Whisk the egg whites in a mixing bowl until they begin to foam and slightly thicken. An electric whisk makes this job much easier if you have one. Sift in the icing sugar, flour and ground star anise, if using, then mix in. Add the ground almonds and lemon zest, then pour in the cooled butter (fish out the whole star anise, if used) and mix until you have a smooth batter. Finally, fold in the blackcurrants, without breaking them up too much.

Scrape the batter into your tin and bake for 60 minutes, or until a toothpick inserted comes out clean. The top of the cake will have formed a lovely golden-brown crust. Leave to cool, then remove from the tin.

To make the icing, add the blackcurrants and lemon juice to a bowl, then mash up the blackcurrants with the back of a spoon or fork. Then, press the mashed fruit through a sieve into a large, separate bowl, remembering to scrape the underside of the sieve to get all the pulp. Sift in the icing sugar, then mix to form a slightly runny purple icing. Pour over the cooled cake so that the icing starts to run down the sides. Add the remaining blackcurrants to the top of the cake for decoration.

NOTES: Try a variation of this cake with redcurrants and swap the star anise for some vanilla paste.

This recipe uses frozen blackcurrants, which you can find in most good supermarkets' frozen fruit section. However, this recipe also works with fresh blackcurrants, but the cake will require less time in the oven – check it regularly after the 45-minute mark.

TOFFEE APPLE CAKE

In the West Country of the UK, apple harvesting really kicks off in the autumn. Windfalls can often be seen in baskets outside people's houses with a sign saying 'Help yourself'. The abundance of fruit is celebrated for Halloween and bonfire night with apples being dipped in a hard crack caramel to make toffee apples, which are the inspiration for this cake. The additional apples for the second part of the bake are an indulgence, and perhaps at more frugal times can be left off, but the caramel lends an element of sticky toffee pudding. Dessert spoons and custard at the ready.

TO MAKE THE CAKE

160g (5½oz) caster (superfine) sugar
100ml (3½fl oz) apple juice
100g (3½oz) butter
75g (2½oz) yogurt
2 eggs
1 teaspoon vanilla paste
150g (5½oz) peeled, cored and diced (about 5mm/¼in) apple (about 2 apples)
200g (7oz) self-raising flour
1 teaspoon baking powder
a pinch of salt

TO MAKE THE CARAMEL

50g (1¾oz) golden (corn) syrup
50g (1¾oz) caster (superfine) sugar
75ml (2½fl oz) double (heavy) cream
a pinch of salt
30g (1oz) butter
2 apples

custard, to serve (optional) – see page 139 for homemade

Preheat the oven to 180°C fan/350°F/Gas 6 and line your 20cm (8in) round tin using the scrunch-up method (see page 11).

In a pan over a medium heat, dissolve the sugar in the apple juice and stir until there's a slight boil. Remove from the heat and add the butter to the pan, mixing until the butter melts. Set aside to cool while you prepare the other ingredients.

In a large bowl, combine the yogurt, eggs and vanilla. Add the diced apple to the bowl and stir it through the mixture.

Pour the melted butter mixture into the bowl with the yogurt, eggs and vanilla and stir to fully combine. Now add the self-raising flour, baking powder and salt and stir until you have a smooth, runny batter. Working quickly, pour into your lined tray and bake for 40 minutes.

While the cake is baking, make your toffee caramel. Heat the golden syrup and sugar in a high-sided, heavy-based pan set over a medium heat until they have melted and the mixture is bubbling. Whisk in the cream and salt, along with 20g (¾oz) of the butter, then increase the heat and keep things bubbling until the caramel becomes a bit darker in colour. Remove from the heat, then whisk in the remaining butter until well combined.

Remove the core of two apples. Slice into thin wedges, leaving the skin on. Place the slices in the caramel and stir so each slice gets fully coated.

Once the cake has had its 40 minutes in the oven, remove and gently tip the slices of apple and caramel over the top. Return the cake to the oven for a further 20 minutes so that the caramel becomes toffee-like and starts to soak into the cake, and the apples begin to cook and caramelize a little.

If you want dark, chewy apples on top, you can bake the cake for a further 10 minutes with the heat turned up to 230°C fan/475°F/Gas 9.

Delicious served with the custard on page 139, or if there's some yogurt left in the tub, a dollop of that on the plate can offset the sweetness for a tangy acid trip.

SEASONAL FRANGIPANE

Here's a cake that can be made year round and reinvented with the seasons. We've used plums as they were available at the time of writing. You can replace them with whatever takes your fancy: head out and forage for some blackberries in late summer or seek out the tartness of rhubarb in the spring. We've found that the tang of blackcurrants is especially good with the smooth almond flavour. The baking timings are really key for this one as you want that frangipane softness, with just the right amount of stability to keep it together until your fork reaches your mouth.

50g (1¾oz) gluten-free plain (all-purpose) flour
210g (7½oz) ground almonds
130g (4½oz) salted butter
105g (3¾oz) caster (superfine) sugar, plus 35g (1¼oz) extra for tossing the plums
3 eggs
1½ teaspoons lemon juice
325g (11½oz) plums, halved, pitted and thinly sliced lengthways
35g (1¼oz) flaked (sliced) almonds

icing (confectioners') sugar, for dusting
clotted cream, to serve (optional)

Preheat your oven to 170°C fan/340°F/Gas 5 and line a 20cm (8in) square tin using the snip method (see page 11).

In a small mixing bowl, whisk together the flour and ground almonds so they are evenly mixed.

Melt the butter in a saucepan over a low heat or in a microwave. Pour this into a large mixing bowl, or the bowl of a stand mixer, and leave to cool.

Add the sugar to the warm butter and mix until it's glossy and the sugar has dissolved. Next, beat in the eggs and the almond and flour mixture, until all the ingredients are well mixed. Scrape the sides and bottom of the bowl, add your lemon juice, and give the mixture one final beat.

In a separate bowl, toss the sliced plums in the remaining sugar, evenly coating all the slices.

Pour the frangipane mixture into your tin and spread it evenly, getting right into the corners. Lay the plum slices evenly on top of the frangipane and sprinkle the flaked almonds across them. Bake for 45 minutes or until the edges begin to brown and come away from the sides.

Once baked, remove from the oven and let it cool for 10 minutes, then remove from the tin and let it cool completely before slicing.

To serve, finish with a generous dusting of icing sugar and even a dollop of clotted cream, if you like.

RETRO
BAKES

We've always loved tinkering with the classic cakes and vintage bakes that bring us those nostalgic feels: the ones that remind us of someone or something and conjure a personal moment or a specific time that most of us can relate to. In this section, we take a trip through time, putting our own spin on the food that honed our taste buds and took us on a cultural journey, from campfire s'mores to school dinner sponge. Hopefully, these recipes and flavours will bring to mind some happy memories for you, and maybe even some stories you'll want to share while scoffing down your own sentimental sweets.

EASY TEA LOAF

Wales has bara brith, Ireland has barmbrack, Scotland has Jock's loaf and England has the tea loaf. They are all in the same recipe family, with many variations out there. Some will lay claim to their family recipe being the best, but we encourage you to use this as your base and add your own personal spin – a touch more cinnamon, a shot of whisky or a particular brand of tea – to begin your own tea loaf legacy. Mixed dried fruit packets from the supermarket are great, but you may want to steer the fruit in a particular direction by blending in some maraschino cherries with a splash of the syrup, for example. Whichever tea loaf you make, we recommend serving with a hearty slathering of butter. If you're feeling extra adventurous, a bit of Cheddar cheese on the side can really work too.

2 tea bags
200ml (7fl oz) boiling water
finely grated zest and juice of
  1 orange
250g (9oz) mixed dried fruit
200g (7oz) soft light brown sugar
2 eggs
300g (10½oz) self-raising flour
1 teaspoon mixed (pumpkin pie)
  spice

Cheddar cheese and butter, to
  serve (optional)

Put your tea bags in a bowl with the boiling water and leave them to steep for 10 minutes, then remove the tea bags and add the orange zest and juice along with the dried fruit. Cover and leave for as long as possible for the fruit to plump up, ideally overnight.

Preheat the oven to 140°C fan/280°F/Gas 3 and line a 2lb (900g) loaf tin using the scrunch-up method (see page 11).

Beat the sugar and eggs in a stand mixer or a large mixing bowl using a wooden spoon, until light and fluffy. Sift in the flour and mixed spice, then add the tea-soaked fruit and mix until fully combined.

Pour into your lined loaf tin and bake for 60–70 minutes, until the top is golden brown and a toothpick inserted comes out clean. If the cake is getting too dark, cover with foil to stop it burning. Leave to cool completely before removing from the tin. Slice and serve with plenty of butter.

NOTES: This recipe really works with lemon too, and we strongly encourage you to create your own spin on this recipe.

You can add a little melted butter or oil to the mix if you prefer a softer crumb.

RASPBERRY & WHITE CHOCOLATE SPONGE

This is like a Victoria sponge sandwich with a contemporary twist. The white chocolate adds a luxurious texture to the cream, adding sweetness against the sharpness of the raspberries. The hint of orange is like a fashion statement to say 'Hey, I'm different', but it also parties hard with the raspberry and white chocolate.

TO MAKE THE FILLING
150ml (5fl oz) double (heavy) cream
75g (2½oz) white chocolate, broken into pieces
½ teaspoon orange extract
200g (7oz) seedless raspberry jam (see page 138 for homemade)
150g (5½oz) raspberries

TO MAKE THE CAKE
200g (7oz) soft butter
200g (7oz) caster (superfine) sugar
1 teaspoon vanilla paste
4 eggs
200g (7oz) self-raising flour
1 teaspoon baking powder
a pinch of salt
finely grated zest and juice of ½ small orange

icing (confectioners') sugar, for dusting

Preheat the oven to 150°C fan/300°F/Gas 3½ and line your 20cm (8in) round tin (see page 11).

Start by making the chocolate orange filling. Warm half the cream in a saucepan until small bubbles start to rise at the edges. Remove from the heat. Place the white chocolate in a large bowl.

Pour the hot cream over the chocolate and gently stir until all the chocolate is melted. Add a few dashes of orange extract and mix until everything is combined into a white chocolate ganache, then place in the fridge until needed.

To make the cake, cream the butter and sugar in a stand mixer or a large mixing bowl using a wooden spoon, until light and fluffy. Add the vanilla and the eggs one by one, mixing well after each addition and scraping down the sides of the bowl.

Sift the flour, baking powder and a pinch of salt into the mix and gently fold in. Add the orange zest and juice and fold to combine.

Gently decant the cake batter into your lined tin and bake for 45–50 minutes, or until the top becomes golden brown and a toothpick inserted comes out clean. Leave to cool in the tin.

Remove the white chocolate ganache from the fridge and add the remaining cream to the bowl. Whisk together until the cream becomes thick and airy. An electric whisk makes this job much easier. If you over mix, a splash of milk can be added to loosen things up again.

Once the sponge is cool, remove it from the tin and slice horizontally to create the two sandwich halves. Spread raspberry jam on the bottom sponge layer, then spread chocolate orange cream on top of the jam. Place fresh raspberries around the edges of the cream layer so they can be seen.

Very carefully place the other half of the sponge on top, being sure to support it underneath as you lift. Dust the top of the cake with icing sugar, slice and serve.

NOTES: The sponge cake is best made fresh but can be made a day ahead or even frozen.

If you don't like orange, some extra vanilla in the cream will work just as well.

THE AMBASSADOR'S LOAF

This will be the pièce de résistance at any state dinner party, wolfed down by seasoned dignitaries. All Ferrero Rocher jokes aside, this is a decadent chocolate and hazelnut sponge, with a cheeky nod towards those iconic adverts. What's not to love?

TO MAKE THE CAKE

100g (3½oz) blanched hazelnuts
180g (6¼oz) butter
225g (8oz) full-fat Greek yogurt
¾ teaspoon bicarbonate of soda
  (baking soda)
3 eggs
180g (6¼oz) caster (superfine)
  sugar
270g (9½oz) self-raising flour
¾ teaspoon baking powder
¾ teaspoon salt

TO MAKE THE GANACHE

90ml (3fl oz) double (heavy) cream
90g (3¼oz) dark chocolate
90g (3¼oz) chocolate hazelnut
  spread (see page 137 for
  homemade)
¾ teaspoon vanilla paste

Preheat the oven to 160°C fan/320°F/Gas 4 and line a 2lb (900g) loaf tin (see page 11).

Start by lightly toasting your hazelnuts in the oven for 10 minutes on a baking tray (sheet pan) until they just start to brown, then set aside to cool slightly. Once cooled, place in a tea towel and bash them up with a rolling pin or whizz them in a food processor until they're all broken into little pieces.

Melt the butter in a saucepan over a low heat, then set aside to cool. Meanwhile, place the yogurt in a bowl with the bicarbonate of soda and beat in the eggs.

Put the sugar in a large mixing bowl, then add the melted butter and mix until the sugar begins to dissolve. Add the yogurt-egg mixture and stir until fully combined. Sift in the flour, baking powder and salt, then fold everything together to form a batter. Finally, fold in most of the broken-up hazelnuts, reserving a small handful for decorating the top of the cake.

Scrape the batter into your lined loaf tin and bake for 45 minutes, or until a toothpick inserted comes out clean. Leave to cool in the tin.

To make the ganache, heat the cream in a saucepan to just before boiling point. Break the chocolate into small pieces and place in a bowl with the hazelnut spread and vanilla. Pour over the hot cream, leave for 1–2 minutes, then mix together until it all melts and forms a ganache. If it doesn't melt fully, you can finish the ganache in the microwave, but only heat it in 5-second bursts so it doesn't split.

Remove the cooled cake from the tin and pour over the ganache, allowing some to spill down the sides of the cake. Finish off by sprinkling the reserved hazelnut pieces on top.

S'MORES CAKE

Everyone knows the joys of sitting around a campfire: telling scary stories, getting smoke in your eyes, and judging the perfect time to remove a smouldering marshmallow from the fire before it burns to a cinder. You may even have trapped this squishy delight between a couple of chocolate biscuits to make a s'more, the perfect campfire snack. Here, we bring that experience into the home, hopefully minus the smoke in the eyes and the inevitable bad guitar-playing.

TO MAKE THE BASE
300g (10½oz) digestive biscuits (graham crackers)
150g (5½oz) butter

TO MAKE THE GANACHE
300g (10½oz) milk or dark chocolate, chopped
150ml (5fl oz) double (heavy) cream

280g (10oz) marshmallows

Line your 20cm (8in) square tin using the snip method (see page 11).

Finely crush the biscuits, either in a food processor, or by placing into a zip-lock bag or tea towel and bashing with a rolling pin.

Melt the butter either in a saucepan over a low heat or in the microwave. Mix with the broken biscuits to form a sort of dough. Press this firmly into the base of your tin using the back of a spoon, then place the tin in the fridge or freezer to firm up.

Now make your chocolate ganache. Place the chopped chocolate in a heatproof bowl. Heat the cream in a saucepan over a medium heat until just before boiling point, then pour it over the chocolate. Leave for 1–2 minutes, then mix until the chocolate is fully melted. If it does not melt fully, pop your bowl over a pan of barely simmering water, ensuring the bowl does not touch the water, and warm the ganache, stirring continuously, until the chocolate is fully melted. When your ganache is ready, remove the biscuit base from the fridge or freezer, pour the ganache over the top and spread into an even layer.

While the chocolate is still soft, press the marshmallows on top to form a layer. Try to squeeze them all in so the ganache is completely covered. Place in the fridge for a couple of hours to set the ganache.

Either using a blow torch or under a hot grill (broiler), toast the marshmallows until they are golden brown. Leave the cake to come to room temperature – you want the marshmallows slightly firmer and the chocolate a little softer – then cut into slices and serve.

NOTES: Try using the Bignob recipe on page 87 for the base.

For something a little different, you could swirl some peanut butter or tahini into the ganache. Alternatively, using a ginger nut biscuit for the base is a good way to spice this up a little.

BIGNOB BISCUIT

This is a homage not just to the nostalgic Hobnob biscuit, but to the simple pleasures in life and the ceremony of having a cuppa. The comedian Peter Kay once described the Hobnob as the Royal Marine of biscuits for its ability to be dunked repeatedly in a cup of tea without breaking. The firm texture of a Hobnob does give it some serious sturdiness. Dunking a slice of this in a hot tea creates an alchemy that elevates this humble biscuit to the realms of fine patisserie. There is an art to dunking, especially when biscuiteers make them wider than a cup. This is why we recommend you cut your biscuit into triangles for an engineered military dunk.

150g (5½oz) butter
2 tablespoons honey or golden (corn) syrup
150g (5½oz) soft light brown sugar
150g (5½oz) rolled oats
150g (5½oz) self-raising flour
1 teaspoon salt

50g (1¾oz) dark or milk chocolate, melted, for drizzling (optional)

Preheat the oven to 180°C fan/350°F/Gas 6 and line your 20cm (8in) round tin (see page 11).

Melt the butter with the honey in a saucepan over a low heat.

Meanwhile, add the dry ingredients to a large mixing bowl and give them a rough mix. Pour in the melted butter and honey and mix until a rough dough forms.

Using your hands or a spatula, evenly press the mixture into your round tin, then bake for 20–25 minutes until golden brown. Leave to cool for 10 minutes, then remove from the tin and mark out triangle slices, like how you'd cut a pizza. Leave to cool completely, then drizzle melted chocolate on top, if you like.

Snap into individual portions when serving. Store in an airtight container for a week or two.

NOTE: You can add chocolate chips to the biscuit mixture or some dried fruit, should you wish to adapt this.

TREACLE PUDDING

All the joys of a treacle tart, with the convenience of a loaf cake. We've even removed the extra job of making and blind baking your own pastry. The big win for this cake is that it is a great way to use up some bin-dodging old bread. Any bread will do, but sourdough will add more depth to an already classic flavour. We feel this isn't just a reinvention of a classic, but a rare case where simplifying something delivers more flavour and complexity than the original.

TO MAKE THE CAKE
100g (3½oz) stale sourdough
  bread
250g (9oz) soft butter
200g (7oz) golden (corn) syrup
4 eggs
finely grated zest and juice of
  1 lemon
150g (5½oz) self-raising flour
½ teaspoon bicarbonate of soda
  (baking soda)
¼ teaspoon salt

TO MAKE THE TOPPING
75g–100g (2½–3½oz) golden
  (corn) syrup
pinch of sea salt flakes

clotted cream or ice cream,
  to serve

Preheat your oven to 170°C fan/340°F/Gas 5 and line your 2lb (900g) loaf tin (see page 11).

Blitz or grate the bread, then add the crumbs to a large mixing bowl. Beat in the butter, golden syrup, eggs and finally add your lemon juice and zest. Next, sift in the flour, bicarbonate of soda and salt and fold everything together to form a batter, then scrape the mixture into your prepared loaf tin.

Bake for 30–45 minutes, depending on how dry your bread is, until the top of the cake is golden brown. Remove from the oven and pour the topping golden syrup over the cake, then return to the oven for another 5 minutes to allow it to soak into the sponge. Remove from the oven, leave to cool slightly and sprinkle with some sea salt flakes. Serve hot with oodles of clotted cream or a couple of scoops of quality ice cream.

NOTES: Often it's just the very end of the loaf that is wasted or goes stale. We suggest freezing these bits if you have the space and that way you can build up a little stash for when you're ready to bake.

You can also dry out the crumbs, which will help extend shelf life - spread them out on a baking tray, then bake in an oven preheated to 160°C fan/320°F/Gas 4 for 10 minutes. Just be sure to add an extra knob of butter to the cake mix to compensate.

JAM SPONGE

This cake always reminds us of the time we mischievously climbed through an open window into the school canteen. One day after hours, we – still in our uniforms – discovered a rack filled with freshly made cakes for the day ahead. We decided to go to town on the jam sponge, but we didn't get far before feeling a bit sick and very guilty, so we skedaddled. We never got caught, but here's a confession for our sins. Sorry to those hard working dinner ladies, who provided us with food most days in our misspent youth. This recipe goes out to you!

TO MAKE THE CAKE
180g (6¼oz) soft butter
180g (6¼oz) caster (superfine) sugar
4 eggs
180g (6¼oz) self-raising flour
½ teaspoon baking powder
¼ teaspoon salt

TO MAKE THE TOPPING
120g (4¼oz) seedless raspberry jam (see page 138 for homemade)
20g (¾oz) desiccated (dried shredded) coconut

tinned custard, to serve

Preheat the oven to 180°C fan/350°F/Gas 6 and line a 20cm (8in) square tin (see page 11).

To make the sponge, cream the butter and sugar in a stand mixer or a large mixing bowl using a wooden spoon, until light and fluffy. Add the eggs one by one, mixing well after each addition and scraping down the sides of the mixing bowl. Sift in the flour, baking powder and salt, then fold in until combined.

Scrape the batter into the lined tin and bake for 25–30 minutes, or until the top is golden and springs back when pressed. Remove from the oven and, still in the tin, spread the jam over the hot cake, then sprinkle over the coconut, making sure to get an even coverage from edge to edge.

Serve warm, school-dinner style, with tinned custard, or leave to cool and serve in slices with a cup of tea when your gran comes to visit.

NOTES: Any jam will do and it doesn't have to be seedless. We just wanted to make something school-canteen style.

It's illegal to serve jam sponge without custard, so don't break the law!

PB&J BLONDIE

The PB&J has universal appeal, cultural iconic status and a sense of fun unrivalled in the sandwich world. This goes for kids and adults alike. The blondie is a little more niche, but still has a sense of playfulness – it's just a massive cookie after all. That's why we thought the two would get along just fine and bring a bit of fun to any gathering. This is a quick-fire method, so no need for chilling down the dough.

150g (5½oz) butter
75g (2½oz) caster (superfine) sugar
75g (2½oz) soft light brown sugar
3 eggs
150g (5½oz) self-raising flour
½ teaspoon salt
150g (5½oz) white chocolate drops or a bar, broken into small pieces
3 tablespoons smooth peanut butter (see page 140 for homemade)
4 tablespoons strawberry jam (jelly)
30g (1oz) roughly chopped peanuts

Preheat your oven to 170°C fan/340°F/Gas 5 and line a 20cm (8in) square tin using the scrunch-up method (see page 11).

Place the butter in a pan over a low heat and cook for about 8 minutes whilst stirring gently. It will start to form brown bits as it caramelizes. Let it foam away until it is chestnut-brown in colour and starts to smell delicious and nutty, then pour into a mixing bowl, including any browned solids, and add the sugars. Beat together so the sugar begins to dissolve. Add your eggs and keep mixing until you have a glossy, smooth mixture.

Sift the flour and salt into the mixing bowl and add the white chocolate drops or pieces. Give it a light mix to form a runny dough.

Scrape the mixture into your tin and spread to level. Using two teaspoons, plonk small dollops of peanut butter and jam on top of the batter, then swirl into patterns using a knife or a cocktail stick. Scatter the peanuts on top and bake for 35 minutes until golden. You want a blondie to be slightly undercooked, so a bit of a wobble in the middle will tell you that it's ready to remove from the oven.

NOTES: When it comes to jam, use whatever you prefer: blackcurrant jam will add a good contrast in colour and bring some welcome acidity to a very sweet bake.

You can also switch out the peanut butter with another nut or seed butter – tahini works a treat!

SOLERO CAKE

When the weather outside is getting you down, the skies are heavy with grey clouds and rain is battering the windows, just flip to this recipe. The sun will pretty much burst off the page and back into your life and the oven will welcome this cake with a deck chair at the ready. Let a little bit of summer in and enjoy this deliciously moist and joyful cake.

TO MAKE THE CAKE

100ml (3½fl oz) rapeseed (canola) oil
100g (3½oz) tinned mango pulp
100g (3½oz) full-fat Greek yogurt
2 eggs
100g (3½oz) tinned pineapple chunks, finely diced
250g (9oz) self-raising flour
160g (5½oz) caster (superfine) sugar
70g (2½oz) ground almonds
2 teaspoons baking powder
small pinch of salt

TO MAKE THE ICING

250g (9oz) chilled mascarpone
2 teaspoons icing (confectioners') sugar, sifted
½ teaspoon vanilla paste

pulp of 3 fresh passion fruits, for decorating

Preheat the oven to 150°C fan/300°F/Gas 3½ and line your 20cm (8in) round tin using the disc method (see page 11).

To make the cake, add the oil, mango pulp, Greek yogurt and eggs to a large mixing bowl and whisk together until all the ingredients are mixed and there are no lumps.

Sift the self-raising flour over the top of the wet ingredients, then add the remaining dry ingredients and whisk everything together until you have a smooth cake mixture. Finally, fold in the diced pineapple.

Pour the cake mixture into the prepared tin and bake for 35 minutes or until a toothpick inserted comes out clean. Allow the cake to cool in the tin for 10 minutes, then carefully remove it and allow to cool completely.

Whilst the cake is cooling, prepare the icing. Place all the ingredients in a stand mixer or a large mixing bowl and whisk until thickened and spreadable. If you don't have a stand mixer, an electric whisk makes this job much easier, or alternatively it may just require some elbow grease.

To serve, dollop the icing on top of your cake and begin by spreading it from the middle of the cake out to the edges. With an offset spatula, create an icing 'moat' around the edge of the cake – this will help keep the passion fruit pulp from escaping. Scoop the pulp of your passion fruits on top of the icing and distribute evenly.

CUSTARD JAM SLICE

The custard slice is an architecturally perfect piece of pastry. The crisp flakiness sandwiches the silky custard in just the right way, adding the perfect amount of texture. The added jam brings some fun to the party, injecting a layer of colour into your otherwise beige masterpiece. If you're looking for a bit more sophistication, the next level addition to this would be to use finely sliced fresh strawberries instead of jam.

2 sheets of shop-bought puff pastry, thawed, if frozen (or make your own; see page 134)
1 jar of strawberry jam (or flavour of your choice)
375ml (13fl oz) whole milk
375ml (13fl oz) single (light) cream
60g (2¼oz) butter, chopped
2 teaspoons vanilla paste
150g (5½oz) caster (superfine) sugar
100g (3½oz) cornflour (cornstarch)
6 egg yolks

icing (confectioners') sugar, for dusting

Preheat the oven to 200°C fan/400°F/Gas 7 and line your 20cm (8in) square tin using the snip method (see page 11).

Line two flat baking trays (sheet pans), big enough to fit your pastry sheets, with greaseproof paper. Lay a sheet of pastry on each one, then top the pastry with another sheet of greaseproof paper and stack another flat tray on top. Alternatively, if you don't have four trays, you can bake them separately. Bake for 20–25 minutes until golden and crisp, then set aside to cool.

Using the base of your lined, square baking tray as a guide, trim the cooled pastry sheets to size. A very sharp serrated knife will work best for this. Place the bottom pastry square into your lined tray and top with a healthy layer of the strawberry jam, spreading it evenly. Put to one side whilst you prepare the custard.

Add your milk, cream, butter, vanilla and sugar to a large pan and set over a medium heat. Allow the ingredients to almost come to the boil, then remove from the heat. In a separate bowl, whisk together the cornflour and 125ml (4fl oz) water until smooth, then add this to the milk mixture, followed by your egg yolks. Put the pan back over a medium heat and bring to the boil, whisking continuously. Once the custard begins to boil it will become very thick but keep whisking vigorously for around 1 minute to cook out the cornflour, then remove from the heat. Immediately pass the custard through a sieve into a jug.

Pour the custard on top of the jam-covered pastry layer in your prepared tin, spreading it evenly into the corners, then lay the other square of pastry on top of the custard and press down gently. Put the tin in the fridge to set for a minimum of 5 hours.

Once set, gently lift the custard slice from the tin, holding onto the parchment paper for support, and place on a chopping board. Dust with icing sugar and cut into portions with a very sharp serrated knife.

NOTE: To make your own raspberry jam for this recipe instead of the strawberry, see page 138.

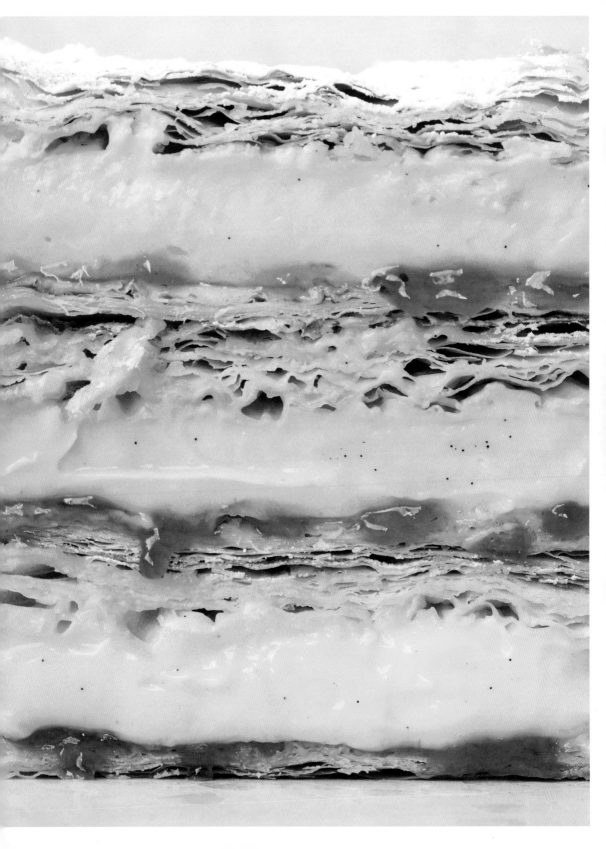

LESS IS MORE

In this chapter, we're not just cutting down on ingredients, we're curating them. We're choosing them with care, handling them with respect, and giving them the space to show off. This isn't about making do with less. It's about achieving more with less. We've even cut the oven out of the equation with some bakeless bakes, because sometimes you don't want to look at your oven - you've been burnt one too many times and it's never even said sorry. A little space is a good thing, giving everyone time to cool off and explore the world of baking without an oven. We also feel that sometimes the best bakes have minimal ingredients when the flavour can be bigger than the sum of their parts, allowing each element to shine.

WHITE BAKED CUSTARD

This is an ode to the egg custard tart. Even the despicable supermarket ones have a place in our hearts, especially when there's a generous grating of nutmeg over the top and they've had a quick blast in the oven to warm them through. This recipe, however, has ditched any form of pastry. It's a lighter version made with egg whites and it's best served chilled – much more suited to the summer and delicious alongside a fruit compote (see page 138) or fresh berries, with a grating of white chocolate.

600ml (21fl oz) double (heavy) cream
140g (5oz) egg whites (about 5 eggs)
60g (2¼oz) caster (superfine) sugar
2 teaspoons vanilla paste
finely grated nutmeg

Preheat the oven to 120°C fan/250°F/Gas 1 and line your 2lb (900g) loaf tin using the scrunch-up method (see page 11).

In a saucepan, heat the cream over a medium heat to just before boiling point, then set aside to cool slightly.

In a mixing bowl, beat together the egg whites and sugar until they just start to form bubbles. When the cream has cooled slightly but is still warm, pour into the bowl along with the vanilla and give it all a good mix.

Pour the contents of the mixing bowl through a sieve into your lined loaf tin. Place the loaf tin in a roasting tray, then fill the outer tray with water so it comes to the same level as the cream mixture inside the loaf tin. Grate a dusting of nutmeg over the top of the custard.

Bake for 60–65 minutes until the cream has a nice wobble and is no longer a liquid, more like a white set jelly.

Place in the fridge or freezer to chill before serving.

NOTE: When heating in a pan, the cream can be infused with various spices, zests, fig leaves, bay leaves and herbs such as lemon thyme, for a subtle complexity. Just strain the cream through a fine sieve when adding to the sugar and egg white mixture.

FLOURLESS CHOCOLATE CAKE

This cake knows how to land a chocolate punch, so if you're ever going to trade up on your chocolate, now is the time to do it. Go for some serious single-origin stuff, 85% cocoa solids if you can handle it – just be sure to leave out the cocoa powder if you wade that far into the chocolatey depths. This cake might cost a little extra, but the result will pay you back with sheer joy.

300g (10½oz) dark chocolate
 (85% ideally)
200g (7oz) butter
20–40g (¾–1½oz) cocoa powder
 (optional; see note)
6 eggs
200g (7oz) soft light brown sugar
¼ teaspoon salt

whipped cream or crème fraîche,
 to serve (optional)
sea salt and unsweetened cocoa
 powder, for dusting (optional)

Preheat the oven to 160°C fan/320°F/Gas 4 and line your 20cm (8in) round tin using the scrunch-up method (see page 11).

Melt the chocolate and butter together in a heatproof bowl over a pan of barely simmering water, ensuring the bowl and water do not touch. If using cocoa powder, add this to your chocolate and butter and mix until any lumps disappear. Set aside to cool slightly.

In a large mixing bowl, whisk the eggs and sugar together until they become pale and frothy and the mixture more than doubles in size. An electric whisk makes this job much easier if you have one. Add the salt, then slowly pour in the melted chocolate mixture and mix until it is smooth and glossy, and all one colour.

Pour into the lined tin and bake for 35–40 minutes. The cake will rise above the rim of the tin but should have a slight wobble. Remove from the oven and leave the cake to cool completely. It will sink a bit, leaving you with a dip in the middle, but that's OK – it makes for a slightly truffly texture.

Delicious served with whipped cream or crème fraîche. A sprinkle of sea salt flakes and a dusting of cocoa will only add to the chocolatey mise en scène.

NOTES: If you can't find any 85% chocolate, you can make up the chocolatey oomph with some added cocoa powder. For 60% chocolate, add 40g (1½oz) cocoa powder, or for 70% chocolate, add 20g (¾oz) cocoa powder.

For a cleaner cut, chill the cake before slicing, but leave the slices to come up to room temperature before eating.

NO-CHURN ICE CREAM

On a bakery research trip to San Francisco, we discovered some life-changing soft-serve frozen yogurt from a Greek restaurant called Souvla, where it's served drizzled with olive oil, honey and a sprinkling of sea salt flakes. This gives it an incredible balance of sour, bitter, salty, creamy and sweet, taking you on quite the journey of flavours, and perfect if you want to serve something a little different after a summer evening dinner party. This is a cheat's version that uses crème fraîche and does away with churning or soft-serve machines. It has a different texture to the original, but if you let it soften a little before scooping out of the tin, you'll get a slightly soft-serve, no-fuss frozen dessert.

600g (1lb 5oz) crème fraîche
80g (2¾oz) caster (superfine) sugar
2 teaspoons vanilla paste
6 egg yolks
50ml (1¾fl oz) runny honey
¼ teaspoon salt
50ml (1¾fl oz) extra virgin olive oil

extra virgin olive oil and sea salt flakes, to serve (optional)

Line your 20cm (8in) round tin using the scrunch-up method (see page 11).

Place all the ingredients in a large saucepan and whisk together over a low heat. Keep whisking until the mixture is hot all the way through and all the ingredients are smooth and combined. Do not boil! Pay attention to the bottom of the pan – this is where the eggs will start to scramble and become lumpy if the heat is too high. Pour into your lined tin, then chill in the freezer overnight.

To serve, remove from the freezer and leave to soften for a few minutes. Then, using a spoon or an ice-cream scoop, if you have one, dig in and scoop out a few balls, or cut slices like a cake. Drizzle with a little extra virgin olive oil and sprinkle with a dash of sea salt flakes.

NOTES: If you do start to cook the eggs and things turn lumpy, turn off the heat, place a stick blender in the pan, blend until smooth and then pass through a sieve into your lined tin.

Top this with the sugared almonds on page 135 for a hint of brittle and a satisfying crunch, if you like.

TIRAMISU

Thankfully, this Italian classic appears to have no definitive recipe, there's just a lot of heated debate without any real evidence on what is absolute. This means things can be a little open to interpretation and the use of instant coffee won't cause every Italian ancestor to turn in their grave. But if you have an espresso machine and a traditional dark-roasted coffee, then chuck in some of the good stuff. Also, a nice dark rum can be used instead of an Italian liqueur. The brittle biscuits come to life with a dousing of these pungent liquids and the mascarpone melds the flavours for a romantic dance off between bitter and sweet. A cake that delivers more flavour with less baking.

2 tablespoons instant coffee
200 (7fl oz) warm water
35ml (1fl oz) Marsala, amaretto
   or Frangelico
500g (1lb 2oz) mascarpone
100g (3½oz) caster (superfine)
   sugar
4 eggs yolks
175g (6oz) lady fingers, savoiardi
   or amaretti biscuits

30g (1oz) grated dark chocolate
   or 2 tablespoons unsweetened
   cocoa powder, for dusting

Line your 20cm (8in) square tin using the snip method (see page 11).

Mix the instant coffee with the warm water in a wide bowl, then pour in your chosen booze and set aside to cool.

Place the mascarpone, sugar and egg yolks in a stand mixer or a large mixing bowl and whisk together well until thickened and beautifully smooth. If you don't have a stand mixer, an electric whisk makes this job much easier. Add a couple of teaspoons of your cooling coffee and give it a further mix.

Dip each lady finger briefly into the espresso and booze mix – they should be moistened but not soggy – and lay them in the bottom of your lined tin; you should use about half of them. You may have to break up some of the lady fingers to get them all to fit in one layer. Spread half of the mascarpone mixture over the top. Add another layer of dipped lady fingers, then spread the remaining mascarpone over the top of these.

Refrigerate the tiramisu for a few hours or overnight, allowing the flavours to blend and the dessert to firm up. Just before serving, grate some dark chocolate on top or dust generously with cocoa powder. This dessert will keep for 3–4 days in the fridge.

NOTES: If you fancy making your own sponge biscuit for this, check out our recipe for Cream Powder Puff Cake on page 128.

If you want to make this booze free, just make a little more coffee and perhaps add some vanilla paste.

FAR BRETON

The simple way this cake is put together makes it seem almost effortlessly chic. There's a simplicity that seems to resonate with the serene countryside of Brittany. Similar to a clafoutis, but more boozy, if you're that way inclined – you could use Calvados or the lesser-known Lambig in keeping with the French theme. Alternatively, try soaking the fruit in some apple juice.

50ml (1¾fl oz) Somerset cider
 Brandy, Morello cherry brandy
 or warm apple juice
50g (1¾oz) prunes, roughly diced
120g (4¼oz) plain (all-purpose)
 flour
80g (2¾oz) caster (superfine)
 sugar
½ teaspoon salt
3 eggs
400ml (14fl oz) whole milk
1 teaspoon vanilla paste
100g (3½oz) salted butter

icing (confectioners') sugar, for
 dusting

Heat your soaking liquor of choice to warm and pour this over the prunes. Leave them to soak whilst you prepare the cake batter.

Preheat the oven to 180°C fan/350°F/Gas 6 and line your 20cm (8in) round tin using the scrunch-up method (see page 11).

Sift the flour into a mixing bowl, then add the sugar and salt. Crack the eggs into the bowl and gently whisk to combine everything.

Heat the milk and vanilla in a saucepan over a medium heat. Make sure that it doesn't boil, then drop the butter in and stir to combine. Once all the butter is melted, remove from the heat and leave to cool down a little. Slowly pour this into the mixing bowl, whisking slowly until you have a smooth batter. Strain the fruit well and gently fold through the mixture.

Pour into your lined tin and bake for around 40–45 minutes until nicely caramelized on top and set in the middle – a toothpick inserted should come out clean. Leave to cool completely before dusting with icing sugar.

PEACH COBBLER

Like a crumble, the joys of a simple cobbler can bring light to the darkest of winter nights or add a sense of heartiness to a blissful summer lunch. The versatility of this cake means you can add an endless number of twists and truly make it your own. Tinned peaches are something that everybody loves, and almost everyone has an old tin kicking around the back of the cupboard, so it's a good place to start. You can also just make this a crumble by leaving out the egg.

2 x 410g (14½oz) tins of sliced peaches (500g/1lb 2oz drained weight) – see note
50g (1¾oz) caster (superfine) sugar, plus 20g (¾oz) for sprinkling the peaches and 20g (¾oz) for the topping
75g (2½oz) self-raising flour
½ teaspoon ground cinnamon
a pinch of salt
100g (3½oz) cold butter, cut into small cubes
1 egg

Preheat your oven to 180°C fan/350°F/Gas 6 and line a 20cm (8in) square tin using the scrunch-up method (see page 11).

Drain the peaches and lay the slices in the base of the lined tin. Sprinkle the peaches with the 20g (¾oz) of sugar (about 2 tablespoons) and set aside.

For the cobbler topping, use a large bowl to toss the flour, 50g (1¾oz) sugar, cinnamon and salt together. Rub the butter cubes into the flour mixture using your fingertips to create something that resembles breadcrumbs. Add the egg and mix until it forms a dough. Alternatively, you can use a food processor to whizz all the ingredients together, then add the egg to form a dough.

Spoon the cobbler mix over the peaches to form little islands. Sprinkle over the remaining 20g (¾oz) of sugar, then bake for 45–50 minutes, or until the topping is golden brown. Leave to rest for 10 minutes, then serve with clotted cream or ice cream.

NOTES: There are so many different fruits that will work in a cobbler - strawberries, gooseberries, quince, rhubarb and summer berries to name a few. If you're using less ripe or more acidic fruits, you may need to adjust the sugar levels and get some of them cooking in the oven while you're assembling the cobbler dough.

Treat the fruit like a jam and add some zest, spices and perhaps a little vanilla to liven things up.

Why not hold on to the syrup from your peaches and make the Tinned Fruit Caramel on page 136?

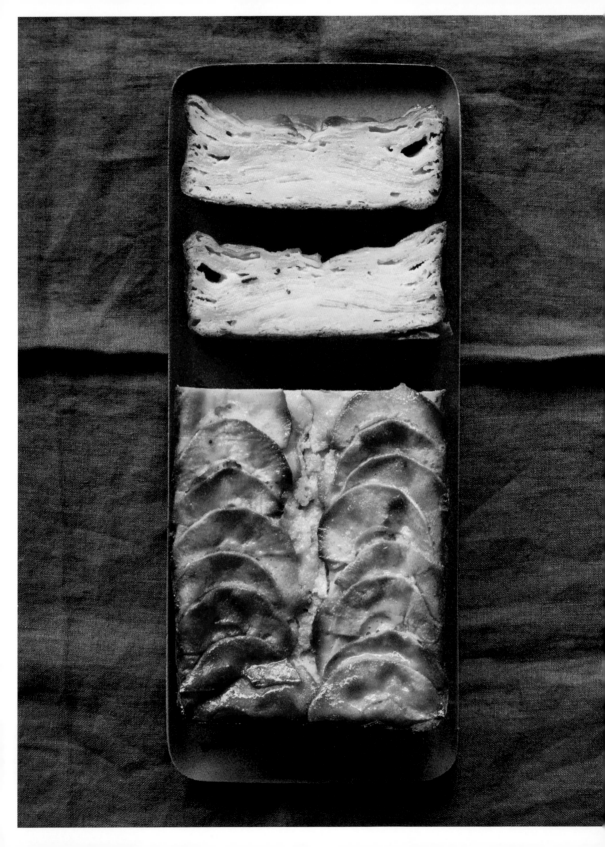

INVISIBLE APPLE CAKE

This is a cake that screams sophistication. It's a classic recipe that needs no tinkering, letting the flavour and copious amount of apples do the talking. As the name suggests, there's a disappearing act that takes place as the thinly sliced apples almost become one with the custardy cake batter, making it a pudding-like cake with hints of apple texture all the way through. A mandolin is perfect for slicing the apples, if you have one.

170g (6oz) plain (all-purpose) flour
1 teaspoon baking powder
30g (1oz) butter, melted
120ml (4fl oz) whole milk
3 eggs
135g (4¾oz) caster (superfine) sugar, plus extra to sprinkle
1.1kg (2lb 7oz) apples (Granny Smith or Pink Lady), peeled, cored and cut into very thin slices (2mm/¹⁄₁₆in)

Maple Syrup Caramel (see page 136), to serve (optional)

Preheat your oven to 190°C fan/375°F/Gas 6-7 and grease and line your 2lb (900g) loaf tin using the strip method (see page 11).

Sift your flour and baking powder into a small bowl and whisk to combine. In another bowl, whisk the melted butter until smooth, then gradually pour in the milk while whisking until everything is well combined.

In a separate mixing bowl, whisk your eggs and sugar together until pale and glossy, or until lifting the whisk leaves a thick ribbon of batter behind. An electric whisk makes this job much easier if you have one. Carefully fold the flour and baking powder into the eggs and sugar until just combined. Add the milk–butter mixture and mix until you have a smooth batter.

Carefully fold the thinly sliced apples into the batter, being careful not to break them and making sure that all the fruit is coated.

Layer up the batter-covered apple slices in your prepared tin, overlapping the slices in a criss-cross fashion. Get them all the way to the edges of the tin, with the straight sides facing outwards, pressing them down lightly as you go. Keep your most-pleasing looking slices for the top layer and, when you get there, arrange in the same criss-cross pattern. Ensure the final layer of apple is not submerged in batter. At this point, there should be around 1cm (½in) to the top of the tin.

Knock the tin on the counter a couple of times to bash out as many air bubbles as you can. Sprinkle the top with a little more sugar, then bake for 50-55 minutes or until the top is a deep golden brown and a toothpick inserted comes out clean.

Leave the cake to cool in the tin for 10 minutes, then transfer to a cooling rack using the parchment paper to lift it, and allow to cool completely.

It's best to chill a little before slicing to ensure you get a clean-looking slice. If serving with the Maple Syrup Caramel, drizzle a pool of caramel on a plate, then place a crisply cut slice of the apple cake on top.

NOTE: It's a good idea to rotate the tin halfway through baking if you can, as the cake can catch on the top and if it is slightly uneven, it cooks unevenly.

PINA COLADA CHEESECAKE

If you like Piña Coladas, then you should listen to this heart-warming tale. During a particularly raucous beachside party some time back in the 80s, this recipe partied so hard it got washed out to sea, where it stayed, drifting, until early 2020. Eventually it washed up on our shore, looking a little worse for wear. We knew exactly what was needed, and rushed it to the nearest beach bar, doused it in rum and pumped up the volume on some Duran Duran. It sprang into life and pretty much danced itself into the baking tin, ready to nourish the life and soul of the party once more.

TO MAKE THE CHEESECAKE
340g (12oz) tinned pineapple, diced into small pieces (fresh is also good if you have it)
finely grated zest and juice of 2 limes
150g (5½oz) caster (superfine) sugar
300g (10½oz) vegan digestive biscuits
100g (3½oz) coconut oil, melted
600g (1lb 5oz) vegan cream cheese
200ml (7fl oz) coconut yogurt
1 teaspoon vanilla paste

TO DECORATE
finely grated zest and juice of 1 lime

Line a 20cm (8in) round springform tin (see page 11).

In a small pan, combine half the pineapple, the lime zest and juice and 2 tablespoons of your sugar and set over a medium heat. Cook, stirring frequently, until the pineapple has started to break down and the sugar and lime have formed a syrup – this should take about 5 minutes. If you're using fresh pineapple, it might take a little longer. Set aside and leave to cool.

Meanwhile, make the cheesecake base. Either place your biscuits into a zip-lock bag or tea towel and smash up using a rolling pin, or pulse into crumbs using a food processor, then transfer to a medium-sized bowl. Add 2 tablespoons of sugar and the coconut oil, then mix until it resembles wet sand. Press this into your lined baking tin, then refrigerate while you finish the filling.

Beat the cream cheese in a large bowl with the remaining sugar until light and fluffy, then add the yogurt and vanilla and beat until the ingredients are combined. An electric whisk makes this job much easier if you have one. Finally, gently fold in your pineapple–lime mixture until just combined.

Pour the filling onto the chilled crust and spread evenly to the edges. Cover and refrigerate for at least 4 hours or ideally overnight.

When you're ready to serve, toss the remaining drained and diced pineapple and lime juice together in a small bowl. Spoon over the cake, then sprinkle with a little fresh lime zest. Cut into slices and serve.

NOTE: Don't discard the syrup from your tin of pineapples. It makes a great Tinned Fruit Caramel – see page 136.

BAKE TO THE FUTURE

If you love to play the gracious host, looking cool, calm and
collected while still delivering the perfect dessert, or you
want to plan a kid's party without the stress, this section is
for you. No matter if you're a seasoned baker or an oven-shy
newbie, prepare to show off your bakes without breaking a sweat.
All the recipes in this section are either made ahead of time
or contain elements that can be pre-prepared or shop-bought to
give you a head-start. And each recipe has an intro to give you
an idea of how to get ahead of your baking schedule, so you can
spend more time schmoozing your guests or putting your feet up.

ICE CREAM SPONGE SANDWICH

While this cake may sound like it's tailor-made to be devoured at a frenzied pace at a kids' party, leaving behind a trail of destruction, faces covered in ice cream and chocolate, and tablecloths strewn with the battle scars of sugar highs past, it's very much the opposite. Cool, calm and composed, it allows the adults to indulge in the flavours of those heady parties on their own terms, with a clean-cut slice of sophisticated decadence. We're talking ice-cream sponge triangle sandwiches for grown-ups. OK, maybe kids too, if they behave. The beauty of this cake is that it can be prepared long before the big party. Why not slice it into portions and wrap them in fancy parchment, ready to serve straight from the freezer?

TO MAKE THE SPONGE

180g (6¼oz) butter, softened
160g (5½oz) caster (superfine) sugar
2 eggs
1 teaspoon vanilla paste
100g (3½oz) natural yogurt
150g (5½oz) self-raising flour
3 tablespoons unsweetened cocoa powder
1 teaspoon baking powder
½ teaspoon salt

TO CONSTRUCT THE CAKE

500ml (17fl oz) tub of shop-bought soft-scoop ice cream
100g (3½oz) seedless raspberry jam (see page 138 for homemade)

icing (confectioners') sugar, for dusting

Preheat the oven to 160°C fan/320°F/Gas 4 and line your 20cm (8in) square tin with parchment paper, leaving some overhang for easy removal (see page 11).

To make the sponge, cream the butter and sugar in a stand mixer or a large mixing bowl using a wooden spoon, until light and fluffy. Add the eggs one by one and keep mixing until smooth, then mix in the vanilla paste and yogurt.

In a separate bowl, sift together the flour, cocoa powder, baking powder and salt. Gradually and gently add these dry ingredients into the wet mixture and mix until just combined, being careful not to overmix.

Pour the batter into the tin and spread it evenly, then bake for 45 minutes or until a toothpick inserted into the centre comes out clean.

Once baked, remove the sponge from the oven and allow it to cool completely in the tin on a wire rack.

Once the sponge has cooled, carefully lift it out of the tin using the parchment paper and place it on a chopping board. Using a sharp knife, slice the sponge in half horizontally to create two thin, square layers. Place both layers in the freezer for an hour or two to firm up. If you are stacking them on top of each other, place some parchment paper between the layers to stop them freezing together.

Remove both layers of sponge from the freezer, and get out your ice cream. First, spread the jam on the cut side of the bottom layer, then when the ice cream has softened slightly, spread it over the cut side of the top layer, using the back of a spoon or spatula to get right to the edges. Flip the bottom sponge layer onto the top, so the jam is sitting on top of the ice cream, then press down gently until the filling is just starting to ooze out. Cover and place in the freezer for around 1 hour until firm, then remove and trim the edges with a sharp knife. Slice into crisp-looking triangle sandwiches and dust with a generous amount of icing sugar.

EASY APPLE CRUMBLE

When the nights draw in and the Sunday roasts get more regular, you know it's the time of year for some crumble. The beauty of this one is that you can make any element of it beforehand. There's no need to even peel your apples – the skin adds some emotional support for the chunks of fruit. You can pre-bake your apples a day or two before, and even leave them in the fridge still in the tin. Baking apples this way creates a beautifully jammy, almost toffee-like texture without the fruit surrendering into a stewed mess. You can then make the rest of the crumble when you're ready and pop it in the oven as you're eating dinner. The result is a more sturdy and grown-up crumble, over the common stewed apple version.

TO COOK THE APPLES
4–6 small eating apples
30g (1oz) butter
75g (2½oz) honey
1 teaspoon vanilla paste
3–4 bay leaves
small pinch of salt

TO MAKE THE CRUMBLE
100g (3½oz) cold butter
100g (3½oz) soft light brown sugar
150g (5½oz) wholemeal flour
50g (1¾oz) sunflower seeds, flaked
   almonds or pine nuts (optional)

yogurt, crème fraîche, cream or ice
   cream, to serve

Preheat the oven to 180°C fan/350°F/Gas 6 and line your 20cm (8in) square tin using the scrunched-up method (see page 11).

Quarter and core the apples, ensuring you remove all the seeds. The easiest way to do this is to cut curved slices from the stalk to the base, retaining as much apple flesh as possible. Leaving the skin intact, place the apples in the tin and add the butter, honey, vanilla, bay leaves and a pinch of salt. Bake for 20 minutes, tossing the apples in the honey mixture halfway. Remove from the oven and discard the bay leaves.

While the apples are baking, prepare the crumble. Cube the cold butter and place in a bowl with the sugar and flour. Using the tips of your fingers, rub it all together until you have something that looks like breadcrumbs. Alternatively, blitz all the ingredients together in a food processor. If you fancy adding a bit more crunch, add the sunflower seeds, almonds or pine nuts. Tip the crumble over the top of the cooked apples and use a spatula to spread the mix out towards the edge of the tin. It doesn't matter if a few apples poke through the crumble.

Return to the oven and bake for a further 30 minutes until the crumble becomes dark golden brown. Serve hot with your favourite dairy – yogurt, crème fraîche, cream or ice cream. Even better eaten cold from the fridge in your dressing gown in the middle of the night!

NOTES: You can also make the crumble topping beforehand – it will keep for up to two weeks in a container in the fridge.

A few rolled oats and a little demerara (turbinado) sugar scattered over the top add a bit more texture.

CARDAMOM CROISSANT LOAF

If you're lucky enough to live near a bakery that makes a good cardamom bun, then you know how delicious they can be, especially with your morning coffee or a small glass of Calvados at Christmas. If you can get your eager hands on some cheap or reduced pre-baked supermarket croissants (it's best to go just before the shop shuts), then try this cheat's version of a cardamom bun. You can get the baking tin filled the night before with a menagerie of croissants and cardamom stickiness, then all you need to do is wake and bake for your pre-prepared breakfast pastry. Using freshly ground cardamom pods is important here to get the best flavour hit, but if you have to use a jar of the pre-ground stuff, then you'll need to add a little extra to compensate for the lack of flavour.

about 30 cardamom pods (to make
  1 teaspoon ground cardamom)
50g (1¾oz) butter
30g (1oz) caster (superfine) sugar
50g (1¾oz) marmalade (see page
  137 for homemade)
100g (3½oz) golden (corn) syrup
6–8 croissants (250–300g/
  9–10½oz)

Preheat the oven to 140°C fan/280°F/Gas 3 and line your 2lb (900g) loaf tin using the scrunched-up method (see page 11).

Bash up the cardamom pods to release the seeds. Discard the husks, then continue grinding to a fine dust using a pestle and mortar, or a spice or coffee grinder will also work. Put about three-quarters in a bowl, keeping the rest for later. Melt the butter and add to the bowl along with the sugar. Mix together to form a wet, sugary emulsion, then add your marmalade and half the golden syrup. Mix until fully combined.

Tear up your croissants, then add them to the bowl with the other ingredients. Using your hands, rub the mixture onto the croissants. Once thoroughly coated, place in the loaf tin as randomly as you like, creating a couple of layers. Use a spatula to scrape any of the remaining mix on top of the croissants.

Cover with foil and bake for 20 minutes, then remove the foil and bake for a further 20 minutes until golden on top. Transfer to a wire rack to cool.

While the loaf is cooling, heat the remaining 50g (1¾oz) of golden syrup in a pan for a few minutes until it starts to boil, then pour over the cooling cake, brushing it into the corners and down the sides of the loaf. Sprinkle with the remaining ground cardamom.

Leave the loaf to cool down – the syrup will soak in and help it to firm up before slicing and serving. Best eaten while guzzling down some delicious coffee.

NOTES: To jazz things up a little, chuck in a few chunks of dark chocolate and finish the loaf with a scattering of crushed, toasted hazelnuts (after the golden syrup).

Alternatively, use the cardamom paste in this recipe to coat 600g (1lb 5oz) frozen croissants (around a dozen), then bake according to the packet instructions on a lined baking tray (sheet pan).

Try using ground cinnamon instead of the cardamom.

SUMMER BERRY TRIFLE

Here's a cake that turns the trifle into a monolith of visual splendour, rather than the more commonly seen colourful mess. It's a simple cake to make, and it brings a layer of considered aesthetic to a classic dessert. Buying the sponge rather than baking it means you're saving time for your future self, with the added bonus of not needing to turn on your oven. This recipe does take a little more brainpower to prepare than the usual method, but we think the payoff is worth it to have a trifle that stands up all on its own. The sherry is a great addition, but if you don't want the alcohol, it's still delicious without.

250g (9oz) Madeira cake
135g (4¾oz) packet of raspberry jelly (jello)
3 tablespoons dry sherry (optional)
200g (7oz) mixed summer berries
2 tablespoons custard powder
1 tablespoon caster (superfine) sugar
200ml (7fl oz) milk
150ml (5fl oz) double (heavy) cream
25g (1oz) icing (confectioners') sugar, sifted
flaked (sliced) almonds (optional)

Line a 2lb (900g) loaf tin using the scrunch-up method (see page 11).

First, boil 250ml (9fl oz) water. While it's heating up, slice the cake into 2cm (¾in) cubes and place loosely in the bottom of your tin.

Cut your jelly into cubes and place in a jug, then pour in the boiling water and stir until fully dissolved. Keep stirring for a while to release some of the heat, then leave to cool for 5–10 minutes.

Splash the sherry over the Madeira cubes, then evenly place the mixed berries on top. If you're using strawberries, it's nice to cut the bottoms flat, then stand them up in a line along the tin. Once the jelly liquid has cooled a little, pour it over the fruit and Madeira cubes, then place in the fridge to set.

To make your custard, place the custard powder and sugar in a small saucepan and whisk them together off the heat, then add a small splash of the milk and keep whisking to form a paste. Turn the hob to a medium heat, pour in the rest of the milk and keep whisking as it heats up. Remove from the heat when it's thickened and forms ribbons when lifted. Transfer to a bowl and press some cling film (plastic wrap) on top so it's touching the custard – this will stop a skin forming. Place in the fridge to chill for 25 minutes.

Meanwhile, in a separate bowl, whip the cream with the sifted icing sugar until it becomes stiff.

Take your loaf tin and custard out of the fridge. The custard should be spreadable at this point – if it looks a little lumpy, just give it a whisk. Spoon into the tin, over the fruit and jelly, then spread with a palette knife to make a flat surface. Finally, dollop the whipped cream on top of this, then spread this flat as well. Pop the whole thing in the fridge to set.

Toast your flaked almonds in a pan until they have a nice colour, moving them around constantly so that they don't catch. Leave to cool, then serve the trifle with almonds sprinkled on top. Make sure to use a super-sharp knife and slice while chilled to get nice clean lines.

NOTE: Try swapping out the Madeira cake for a lemon drizzle loaf. Or if you're really feeling committed, bake your own using the Cream Powder Puff Cake on page 128.

WALNUT & CARAMEL TART

A classic French-style tart with bitter notes from the walnuts offset by sweet caramel to create something deep and meaningful. It's essentially a caramel brittle baked onto pastry, so there's no reason you can't add some extra seeds. Shop-bought pastry is OK here as we feel the heart of this tart lies in its filling.

plain (all-purpose) flour, for dusting
500g (1lb 2oz) shortcrust pastry
300g (10½oz) caster (superfine) sugar
200ml (7fl oz) double (heavy) cream
40g (1½oz) butter
1 teaspoon vanilla paste (or try something boozy)
small pinch of salt
200g (7oz) walnuts or a mixture of flaked almonds, pecans, hazelnuts or pistachios

cream or crème fraîche, to serve

Preheat the oven to 180°C fan/350°F/Gas 6 and line a 20cm (8in) square tin (see page 11).

Roll out your pastry on a floured surface to make a 25cm (10in) square. Roughly place this into your lined baking tin, then lay some parchment paper on top of the pastry. Fill with baking beans (dried rice or lentils will also work) and blind bake for around 15 minutes, then carefully remove the paper and beans and bake for a further 5 minutes.

While the pastry is baking, prepare your filling. Add the sugar and 80ml (2½fl oz) of water to a saucepan and set over a medium heat, stirring until the sugar dissolves. Once it has dissolved, leave things alone, except to give the pan a gentle swirl to make sure the caramel doesn't burn. When the caramel has turned a deep, chestnut brown colour, slowly pour in the cream and stir gently to avoid it splitting. Stir in the butter, vanilla and salt, then add the nuts.

Once the pastry is blind baked, pour the filling on top and return to the oven for a further 30 minutes. You want the caramel to enthusiastically erupt and be bubbling on top. Remove from the oven and leave to cool in the tin before slicing and serving with a dollop of cream or crème fraîche.

NOTES: To make your own sweet-as-a-nut shortcrust pastry, please visit page 134.

This recipe works best in the square baking tin, but you can use the round one too.

CREAM POWDER PUFF CAKE

We've wrestled a classic cream powder puff recipe into a quick and easy, one-pan version, giving it a slight Victoria sponge feel. You'll need to think ahead as this cake is at its best the next day, so we always recommend making it the day before, if you can. The scone-like texture is transformed after being in the fridge overnight, giving a soft, light bite. A Devonshire cream tea with a difference.

TO MAKE THE CAKE

4 eggs
200g (7oz) caster (superfine) sugar
1 teaspoon vanilla paste
100g (3½oz) plain (all-purpose) flour
80g (2¾oz) cornflour (cornstarch)
1 teaspoon bicarbonate of soda (baking soda)
⅛ teaspoon salt

TO MAKE THE FILLING

30g (1oz) caster (superfine) sugar
1 teaspoon vanilla paste
75ml (2½fl oz) sour cream
150ml (5fl oz) double (heavy) cream
1 teaspoon rose water (optional)
about 150g (5½oz) strawberry jam

icing (confectioners') sugar, for dusting

Preheat the oven to 160°C fan/320°F/Gas 4 and line your 20cm (8in) round tin (see page 11).

To make the cake, separate your egg whites and yolks and place the whites in a large mixing bowl with the sugar. Whisk until the egg whites reach soft peaks – it will look like a glossy white emulsion. An electric whisk makes this job much easier. Keep mixing and add the yolks and vanilla until they're all combined.

Sift the flour, cornflour, bicarbonate of soda and salt into the egg mixture and fold very gently to keep all the air in the mixture. Do not over mix!

Very gently transfer the mixture to your baking tin, trying not to knock any air out. Bake for 45 minutes, turning the cake halfway through cooking, until a toothpick inserted comes out clean. It should become a pleasant beige brown when cooked.

Leave to cool, then remove from the tin and transfer to a work surface.

Next, make the cream filling by whipping the sugar, vanilla and sour and double creams in a mixing bowl until they become thick. If you overmix it will get grainy, but a splash of milk can remedy this.

If using the rose water, add it to the strawberry jam in a small bowl (it will help bring out the floral notes of the strawberries).

Slice your cooled sponge horizontally to make two halves for your sandwich. Spread the cream on the cut side of the bottom layer and the jam on the cut side of the top. Then assemble the sandwich by carefully placing the top on the bottom and place in the fridge for a few hours, preferably overnight.

Remove from the fridge about an hour before you want to serve and apply a liberal dusting of icing sugar before slicing.

NOTE: To make your own raspberry jam to use in this recipe instead of the strawberry, see page 138.

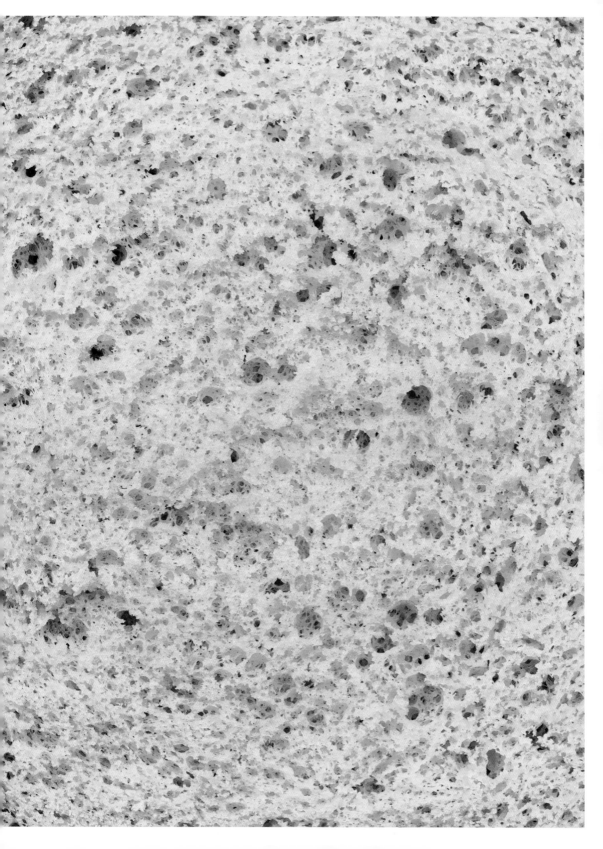

FINANCIER LOAF

A financier is a delicious, simple sponge made with brown butter and lots of ground almonds, but without the bells and whistles of added fruit and chocolate usually found in the closely related friand. Obviously, you're the boss of your own baking destiny, so if you don't want to adhere to tradition, jazzing things up with the addition of some raspberries or white chocolate is fine with us. One of the most delicious bits of gossip about this cake is that it tastes unquestionably better if the batter is left in the fridge overnight to come to terms with its fate. So, think ahead and make the mixture the day before you want to bake.

200g (7oz) salted butter
180g (6¼oz) egg whites (about 6 eggs)
200g (7oz) icing (confectioners') sugar, plus extra for dusting
75g (2½oz) plain (all-purpose) flour
200g (7oz) ground almonds
30g (1oz) flaked (sliced) almonds

Place the butter in a pan over a low heat and cook for about 10 minutes whilst stirring gently. It will start to form brown specks as it caramelizes. Let it foam away until it is chestnut-brown in colour and starts to smell delicious and nutty, then remove from the heat and set aside to cool a little, while remaining melted.

In a mixing bowl, beat your egg whites until they start to foam and slightly thicken. Sift in the icing sugar and flour and mix a little more to combine. Now add the ground almonds and lightly mix them in. Pour in the cooled butter and mix until you have a smooth batter, then cover and place in the fridge for at least an hour to rest, preferably overnight.

Shortly before you are ready to bake the sponge, remove the batter from the fridge and allow to come up to room temperature. Preheat the oven to 170°C fan/340°F/Gas 5 and line your 2lb (900g) loaf tin (see page 11).

Gently scrape the cake batter into the tin and sprinkle with the flaked almonds. Place in the oven and bake for 50 minutes, or until a toothpick inserted comes out clean and the top is golden brown.

Leave to cool completely, then remove from the tin and serve.

NOTE: If you're adding other ingredients such as chocolate or fruit, you may need to make the mix a little drier. Try adding a tablespoon of both ground almonds and flour to balance out the additional wetness.

EASY
EXTRAS

Here's where you can indulge your nerdy side. Get all your
kitchen tools and gadgets out and have some fun with the
fancier flourishes that adorn many of the recipes in this
book. It's also where you'll find the details of some of
the extra toppings and techniques we've used. If there's a
recipe with a shop-bought custard, caramel or curd, this is
the part where you can make the real deal. Although this
book is crammed full of shortcuts and easy wins, these
recipes allow you to take the scenic route and spend a
little more time on your creations, if you so desire. They
also allow you to replenish your store cupboard with jams
and nut butters, or to stock up on the finishing touches,
like candied nuts, that you can use again and again.

SWEET SHORTCRUST PASTRY

Poor old shortcrust seems to have been overshadowed in recent times since laminated pastries have been stealing the show. But shortcrust still has a key role to play. A crumbly, snappy crust can cradle many wonders, from custard and ganache to nutty caramel (see page 127). The added almonds are the key to making this a standout pastry, melting even the coldest of hearts.

MAKES ABOUT 390G (13¾OZ) PASTRY
100g (3½oz) cold butter, cut into small cubes
50g (1¾oz) icing (confectioners') sugar
125g (4½oz) plain (all-purpose) flour
50g (1¾oz) ground almonds
a pinch of salt
1 egg yolk

Place the butter in a bowl with the sugar, flour, ground almonds and salt. Use the tips of your fingers to rub the butter into the dry ingredients until you have something that resembles breadcrumbs. Add the egg yolk and, using a fork, bring the pastry together until a ball of dough forms. If it feels a little dry and crumbly, keep mixing and add cold water, a tablespoon at a time, until it comes together. Alternatively, blitz in a food processor to form the crumbs, then add the egg yolk to form a dough.

Wrap your dough in clingfilm (plastic wrap) and place in the fridge until you're ready to use it (it will keep for 3–4 days). Using a rolling pin and a dusting of flour, roll it to a thickness of about 3mm (⅛in).

NOTE: You can scale up the recipe using the same ratio of ingredients and freeze in portions, then defrost in the fridge when needed.

ROUGH PUFF PASTRY

OK, there's no denying that the easiest way to make puff pastry is to not bother, and to just buy it instead. However, you're reading this recipe, so you must be one of the rare few who have the courage and tenacity to become a pastry aficionado. We take our hats off to you. This labour of love requires a bit of rolling, folding and chilling to create all the buttery layers, but all that huffing and puffing will blow you away when you witness the magic of how seriously flaky pastry is formed.

MAKES ABOUT 625G (1LB 6OZ) PASTRY
250g (9oz) plain (all-purpose) flour
1 tablespoon caster (superfine) sugar
½ teaspoon sea salt
250g (9oz) cold butter

Place your flour, sugar and salt in a large mixing bowl. Grate your cold butter into the mixing bowl with a coarse grater and gently mix into the flour and sugar.

Measure out 150ml (5fl oz) of water into a jug. Pour 6 tablespoons of the water over the mixture and fold until it clumps together. Continue adding water, a tablespoon at a time, until a loose and crumbly dough forms – you may not need it all. Gently knead the dough a few times in the bowl until it becomes smooth, then shape into a rectangular block. Wrap in cling film (plastic wrap) and chill for 1 hour in the fridge.

On a lightly floured surface, roll the chilled dough out to a 1cm (½in) thick rectangle. Fold the dough in thirds like a letter. Turn 90 degrees.

Repeat the rolling, folding and rotating process three more times. Wrap tightly, then chill for at least 2 hours before use.

NOTES: This will keep for 3 days in the fridge, or frozen and defrosted as needed.

This recipe can be used for the Custard Jam Slice on page 96.

CARAMELIZED COCONUT FLAKES

This is an underrated and very quick way to give some texture to your flaked coconut. It gives it a little glow up, adding some colour and sweetness. It's great for topping cakes and flapjacks, but also for pepping up your granola or sprinkling on your morning fruit and yogurt.

MAKES ENOUGH TO TOP 2 OR 3 CAKES
70g (2½oz) coconut flakes
20g (¾oz) maple syrup
¼ teaspoon sea salt
½ teaspoon vanilla paste

Preheat the oven to 170°C fan/340°F/Gas 5.

To make the caramelized coconut, mix all the ingredients together in a mixing bowl, then spread the mixture onto a baking tray (sheet pan) lined with parchment paper. Place the tray in the oven for 7–10 minutes or until the coconut has turned golden brown and is crisp in texture. Be sure to turn the mixture halfway through, so the coconut bakes evenly and doesn't catch.

Kept in an airtight container. It should hold onto its crunch for a week or more.

NOTE: Ideal to use to top our Hummingbird Cake (see page 55), plus many more.

SUGARED ALMONDS

The smell of nuts caramelizing in sugar is one of celebration. Often this style of nut is served in bustling locations, where the sound of carnival combines with the nutty, sweet aroma in the air. If you have those nostalgic memories of nuts being served at your local fair, this recipe will bring all that into your kitchen. It works for all nuts and they add a pleasant brittle crunch to the top of any cake, but they're also delicious on their own.

MAKES ABOUT 250G (9OZ) ALMONDS
200g (7oz) whole almonds (skin on)
100g (3½oz) caster (superfine) sugar
pinch of ground cinnamon

Put all the ingredients in a non-stick frying pan with 2 tablespoons of water and place over a medium heat, stirring continuously. The sugar will melt into the water and become runny at first, but keep stirring until all the liquids have disappeared and the sugar crystallizes and sticks to the almonds. It will have a sandy texture. Reduce the heat to low and cook for a further couple of minutes.

Tip the almonds onto some parchment paper and separate out so that they don't stick together. Leave to cool, then store in an airtight container. They will keep for a few weeks.

NOTE: These nuts can be used to top most cakes, either whole or chopped up. We like them scattered over the Gooseberry Cake (see page 68) or on the No-Churn Ice Cream (see page 104).

MAPLE SYRUP CARAMEL

A deliciously complex syrup reduced down a little for deep, nutty flavours, then lifted up again with a touch of cream. A word of warning: this caramel pairs well with most sweet bakes, with the exception of citrussy ones. However, the acidity in apples joins forces with the maple to score a big flavour goal, so this is ideal served with the Invisible Apple Cake (see page 113) or any cake containing cinnamon, banana, dried or stewed fruits, vanilla or nuts, especially pecans.

MAKES 1 SMALL JAR CARAMEL
330ml (11¼fl oz) maple syrup
3 tablespoons double (heavy) cream

Preheat the oven to 170°C fan/340°F/Gas 5.

Heat the maple syrup over a medium heat in a small pan without stirring. Leave to bubble in the pan for about 10–15 minutes, then remove from the heat and carefully add the cream, stirring gently until fully incorporated.

The caramel can then be stored in a sealed jar or container in the fridge for 2–3 weeks. Reheat briefly in the microwave before serving, if needed.

TINNED FRUIT CARAMEL

Rather than discarding the syrup from your tinned fruit, here's a frugal, creative way to make a super-quick caramel and grab some of that fruit flavour. The syrup in tinned fruit is usually grape juice from concentrate, so there's a bit of acidity. It certainly works for peaches, pears and pineapple and we're sure you can get something fun out of cherries too. If you're making the Peach Cobbler (see page 110), then give this recipe a whirl.

MAKES 1 SMALL JAR CARAMEL
150g (5½oz) caster (superfine) sugar
150ml (5fl oz) tinned fruit syrup
50g (1¾oz) butter
a pinch of salt

Set a clean, dry pan over a medium heat and add the sugar. Leave it to melt for about 5 minutes, until it turns a chestnut brown colour. Don't be tempted to stir the sugar, just tilt the pan and give a gentle swirl if needed.

Once the caramel is dark enough, pour in the strained syrup from the tin of fruit, whisking as you go. It tends to seize up, but trust the process and let things bubble away, continuing to stir so the seized toffee melts back into the liquid. After about 10 minutes, reduce to a low heat and stir in the butter and salt. Remove from the heat and whisk together to form a glossy caramel.

You can use this cold or warm. Either pour directly over your chosen bake, or pour into a jar and place in the fridge until needed. This keeps for up to a month in the fridge.

HAZELNUT CHOCOLATE SPREAD

Making your own hazelnut chocolate spread may seem totally bonkers, as the shop-bought stuff is so delicious, but this recipe ditches the palm oil and the unholy ratio of sugar and forms a real nut butter, with some chocolatey oomph. It doesn't disappoint, and hopefully you'll never look back.

MAKES ABOUT 500G (1LB 2OZ) SPREAD
400g (14oz) blanched whole hazelnuts
40g (1½oz) caster (superfine) sugar
½ teaspoon salt
1 teaspoon vanilla paste
100g (3½oz) dark chocolate, melted

Preheat the oven to 180°C fan/350°F/Gas 6.

Roast the hazelnuts on a baking tray (sheet pan) for 10–15 minutes, until golden, checking them every 5 minutes or so. Once golden, transfer them to a blender while they're still hot.

Blitz the hazelnuts for a few minutes until they turn into a paste. You may need to scrape the sides of the blender intermittently.

Next, add the sugar, salt and vanilla, and blend again until everything is mixed. Finally, add the melted chocolate and blitz once more, then store in a clean sterilized jar (see page 17) or container at room temperature for up to 3 weeks.

NOTES: A powerful blender such as a Nutribullet works well for this recipe but isn't essential. A regular blender may just take a bit longer to make the spread.

If you can only get hold of hazelnuts with their skin on, roast as above, leave to cool slightly then rub them in a tea towel to remove the skins.

This spread is perfect for the Ambassador's Loaf on page 82.

SHORTCUT MARMALADE

This recipe takes a lot of the time and faff out of traditional recipes, without too much compromise. Marmalade is just an orange preserve with a hint of sophistication, where the rind adds a bitterness that sets it apart from the sweetness of jams. It's a great way to use up ageing citrus fruits, and keeps well in a sterilized jar.

MAKES ABOUT 500G (1LB 2OZ) MARMALADE
300g (10½oz) oranges (mandarins or satsumas will also work)
½ lemon
200g (7oz) caster (superfine) sugar

Scrub your oranges and lemon in some warm water to remove any wax, then peel to remove the rind. Finely slice the rind into strips, then place in a large saucepan with 240ml (8fl oz) of water and bring to the boil. Cover with a lid, then turn the heat down to low and allow to simmer for 20 minutes. Make sure it does not boil dry – top up with a little more water if needed.

Meanwhile, finely dice the pulp of the orange and lemon half. Once the rind has finished simmering, add the sugar and chopped pulp to the pan. Increase the heat to high and stir until the sugar has dissolved. Leave the mixture to boil for around 10 minutes, stirring occasionally. Place a small spoonful of marmalade on a chilled plate. Leave it for a second, then give it a push with your finger to see if it creates a wrinkle. If not, keep cooking for a further 5–10 minutes and repeat the test.

Pour the marmalade into a sterilized jar (see page 17) and place a lid on whilst it's still hot.

NOTE: You can use this marmalade in the Cardamom Croissant Loaf (see page 122) or Chocolate & Marmalade Cake (see page 42).

CHERRY COMPOTE

Compote is just jam for grown-ups and can be made with most fruit. The sugar is there to season the fruit and balance any sharpness – it will bring some preserving qualities, but nothing like jam, so this needs to be kept in the fridge and eaten within a week. It's delicious on cakes as well as porridge, granola or simply served in a bowl with cream or ice cream as dessert. The ratio of sugar is all dependent on the fruit you use and your preference for sweetness. Sometimes a little water is needed to break the fruit down at the start of cooking, especially if the fruit is unripe or on the hard side of forgiving.

MAKES 1 SMALL JAR COMPOTE
400g (14oz) fresh or frozen sour cherries
100g (3½oz) caster (superfine) sugar

Place the cherries and sugar into a saucepan and bring to a gentle simmer for 8–10 minutes, stirring constantly until it has reduced and thickened. If you are using frozen fruit, the compote may take a little longer to reduce down.

Put the compote to one side to cool. Store in a sealed jar or airtight container in the fridge and eat within one week.

NOTES: This is delicious served with our White Baked Custard recipe (see page 100).

Sometimes a little spice can get your compote in a hot flush. Try plopping in a cinnamon stick or some star anise to bring a little fun into the baking boudoir.

This recipe will also work with regular cherries (and lots of other soft fruits), but you'll need to reduce the sugar to 50g (1¾oz) to suit the sweetness of your fruit.

RASPBERRY JAM

We've been making this jam for years in our cafe and it's a real crowd-pleaser, especially when served with croissants. If you have a real aversion to seeds, simply sieve them out while the jam is hot. Out of season we use frozen raspberries, which still brings great results. You can use jam sugar that contains pectin if you prefer a more set jam. We like ours a little runny so don't add any, making it all the better for spreading on a buttery pastry.

MAKES ABOUT 450G (1LB) JAM
350g (12oz) fresh or frozen raspberries
350g (12oz) granulated or caster (superfine) sugar

Place your raspberries in a saucepan over a low heat, stirring them so they break up a little and release some juice. If they're frozen, you may need to leave them a little longer to start breaking down. Add the sugar and stir again to release more juices and fully combine the sugar.

Turn the heat up to medium and leave the pan for a few minutes for the sugar to fully dissolve, then stir again – you should have a runny red jam at this stage. Keep cooking, stirring continuously, for about 20 minutes. Test the jam is ready by putting a small spoonful on a chilled plate. Leave it for a second, then give it a push with your finger to see if it creates a wrinkle. If not, keep cooking for a further 5–10 minutes and repeat the test.

Once the jam is ready, pour into a sterilized jar (see page 17) and place the lid on while still hot.

NOTES: Try using the jam in the Raspberry and White Chocolate Sponge (see page 81), Jam Sponge (see page 91) or even our Ice Cream Sponge Sandwich (see page 118).

A little vanilla paste or citrus zest and juice will add some jazzy complexity to your jam.

LEMON CURD

This zingy lemon custard is a spreadable ingredient that originated about 200 years ago in England. It can be liberally applied to toast but also works as a killer ingredient for baking – drizzled on top of cakes or mixed into icings, used for filling tarts or doughnuts, or even baked on top of cookies where it sets into a firm jelly consistency. There's bags of flavour at play with this type of curd and it'll bring a satisfyingly creamy texture to anything in the crumbly cake category.

MAKES 1 JAR CURD
2 medium eggs
1 egg yolk
100ml (3½fl oz) lemon juice
150g (5½oz) caster (superfine) sugar
190g (6¾oz) butter, cut into cubes

Bring a pan of water to the boil. Meanwhile, put the eggs, egg yolk, lemon juice and caster sugar in a heatproof mixing bowl and whisk by hand until all the ingredients are thoroughly combined. Reduce the heat to a gentle simmer and place the bowl on top of the pan, ensuring the water doesn't touch the bowl.

Gently heat the curd, stirring occasionally with a spatula, until it thickens. The curd on the edges of the bowl may thicken quicker, so be sure to scrape down the sides.

Once the curd has a jelly-like 'wobble', add the butter and continue to stir until the butter is fully melted. Give the curd one last mix to make sure it's thoroughly combined and silky smooth.

Transfer to a sterilized jam jar (see page 17) or an airtight container. You can store it in the fridge for up to 2 weeks.

NOTE: Use the lemon curd in our Brown Butter, Lemon & Raspberry Cake (see page 27).

CRÈME ANGLAISE (CUSTARD)

This is more than just posh wording for custard, it's actually a pouring sauce that can be served hot or cold with cake or even churned into ice cream.

MAKES ABOUT 250ML (9FL OZ) CUSTARD
200ml (7fl oz) double (heavy) cream
50ml (1¾fl oz) whole milk
½ teaspoon vanilla paste
25g (1oz) caster (superfine) sugar
3 egg yolks

Over a medium heat, warm the cream and the milk in a pan with the vanilla paste and half of the sugar – it does not need to boil.

Meanwhile, in a bowl, whisk together the egg yolks and remaining sugar by hand until they turn slightly pale in colour. An electric whisk makes this job much easier if you have one. Pour a third of the warm cream into the egg and sugar mixture and whisk well, then add the remaining cream and whisk all the ingredients together. Pour the custard back into the saucepan.

Turn the heat down to low and stir the custard constantly with a spatula. It is ready when it has thickened – this will take about 5 minutes.

Strain the custard through a sieve into a jug and cover it with cling film (plastic wrap), ensuring it touches the surface to stop a skin forming.

NOTES: Serve alongside our Toffee Apple Cake (see page 72), Jam Sponge (see page 91) or Peach Cobbler (see page 110).

To transform this recipe into a baked custard, add a little thickening agent by adding 1 teaspoon of cornflour (cornstarch) or an extra egg yolk, but don't add more than that as you still want that silky texture and a slight wobble after baking.

HOMEMADE PEANUT BUTTER

It's common knowledge that peanut butter accounts for 90 per cent of double dipping and spoon licking. You can make the stuff by just blending peanuts on their own, but the added liquid from the oil makes this easier in the heat of the blender (it will firm up again as it cools). This makes a nut butter that's great spread on hot toast (try a little cracked black pepper on there too), dolloped into banana milkshakes or as an ideal addition to many bakes. A spoonful added to most curries will give a couple of revs on the flavour engine too.

MAKES 1 SMALL JAR
200g (7oz) blanched peanuts
3 tablespoons neutral oil
1 tablespoon honey
pinch of sea salt

Preheat the oven to 160°C fan/320°F/Gas 4.

Place the peanuts on a tray, then bake in the oven for 10–15 minutes until they start to turn golden brown. Add to a blender or food processor while still warm along with all the other ingredients, then blend until smooth and buttery.

Store in a clean, sterilized jar (see page 17) or container at room temperature for up to 3 weeks. You can store your peanut butter in the fridge for up to 3 months, but it may need a good stir before eating again!

NOTES: Try using this in our PB&J Blondie recipe (see page 93).

You can use dry roasted peanuts and skip straight to the blending part, but these shop-bought packets are often coated in lots of other ingredients and may not be suitable for baking. Just read the ingredient list on the packet first.

SEED BUTTER

Gone are the days when seed butters lounged on the shelves of dusty health food shops, perused by the occasional trustafarian. Now, the wellness brigade has their yoga death grip on every jar and for good reason. No longer the poor cousin of the populist nut butters, seed butters are a stylish, sophisticated ingredient in their own right. The creamy texture and subtle flavours have brought things like tahini into the spotlight as a stand up ingredient welcome in any baker's pantry, as they mutter 'namaste' under their buttery breath.

MAKES 1 JAR
500g (1lb 2oz) pumpkin seeds or hulled sunflower seeds
7 tablespoons sunflower oil
2 tablespoons caster (superfine) sugar
a pinch of salt

Preheat the oven to 160°C fan/320°F/Gas 4.

Lay your seeds on a tray and toast in the oven for 5 minutes. Give them a shake so the seeds turn, then give them another 5 minutes until the seeds are just starting to brown. Transfer to a blender or food processor while still hot and whizz away.

Blend for about 5 minutes, scraping down the sides of the blender every so often.

Add the oil, sugar and salt and blend for a further few pulses until it has a smooth, spreadable consistency. You may need to pause if the motor is getting too hot. If the mixture isn't spreadable after the second blend, you can add a touch more oil.

Transfer to a sterilized jar (see page 17) or tub and pop in the fridge until you need it. The butter will keep chilled for up to a month.

NOTES: Try spreading this on slices of Easy Tea Loaf (see page 78).

Why not try this instead of the nut butter in the PB&J Blondie (see page 93)?

The colour from the deep green pumpkin seeds combined with the purple Cherry Compote (see page 138) will look dazzling.

INDEX

ACKNOWLEDGEMENTS

SOME WORDS FROM TOM

Thank you to my partner, Emily, for your precise proofreading, perfectly timed cups of tea and cake critiques that are somehow both gentle and merciless. Your pep talks guide me through the murky waters of imposter syndrome and your big smile gets me through even the toughest of days.

And to Kingsley, this book's dedicated companion. You sit in your chair, silently judging me with disapproving looks or rubbing your pungent beard against my face while I try to type. But that's OK, because you're a dog, blissfully unaware of deadlines, publishing deals or the pressures of success. You just want to be present with those you care about, and that reminds me to do the same.

SOME WORDS FROM OLIVER

Big thanks to my daughter Agatha. You give me so much creativity and confidence, especially when you took our first book into school for your 'Show and Tell' class. I try to see the world through your eyes – it keeps my cynicism at bay and helps me look for the good in the world. Also, to my wonderful wife, who listens to me waffling continuously about all the good and bad in my day to day; you are the best pair of ears in the world. I dedicate this book to Ernest (my cat). It's a bit tongue in cheek, but our pets do provide so much joy and relieve so much stress. Ernest makes me laugh multiple times a day, and on those bad days, a quick cuddle or putting my face in his soft tummy provides comfort like no other.

SOME WORDS FROM US BOTH

We have so much gratitude to everyone who bought the first book. Without such unexpectedly good sales, the publisher would not have picked up the phone to offer us this next one.

If you do want us to write a third book, then all of you need to go out and buy multiple copies of this one: give them as presents; use them as door stops for all we care! On a serious note, it was our commissioning editor, Stacey Cleworth who made this book happen. Thanks for all your guidance,

having the vision and giving us the encouragement we needed to put pen to paper. You're such a talent and someone as young as you has a great career in publishing ahead, even though you've achieved so much already. To the whole team at Quadrille, who created a rock solid foundation to make this happen, thank you all.

Sam Harris, with your impeccable photography, we are so privileged to have someone of your calibre shoot our scruffy cakes. You've become a good friend and I hope we continue eating delicious dinners with you and sampling fine wines, or at least grabbing the odd pint of ale at the St John bar. Matthew Hague, for assisting Sam, even though you're a fully fledged food photographer, we were so pleased you came back to help out on this book. Becks Wilkinson, for the food styling and making the cakes, but really you did so much more – the ink was barely dry on our rag tag manuscript and you navigated it so well. You're a force of nature, with some seriously good vibes. Thanks to Valeria, who never stopped working all day, sometimes juggling cakes between three ovens whilst washing up and icing cakes at the same time. Max, the prop stylist, for the big hugs on meeting you. You clearly have a big heart and an eye for choosing the best selection of kitchenalia. Also, thanks for bringing your personal items from home and the most magical selection of tablecloths and fabrics. Your style and warmth is clearly woven throughout Sam's images. This cookbook, like many others, is a big collaboration with so many people working overtime to create lots of elements that a reader may not see or know about. The authors may have their name on the front, but the book wouldn't happen without a great team behind the pages.

Speaking of teams, we owe so much to our bunch at the Exploding Bakery, who made it possible for us to take enough time out of the company to write this. Without you all crewing the ship and keeping it afloat in our absence, there would be no book.